CONTENTS

EDITORIAL FOREWORD

Such is the pace of historical enquiry in the modern world that there is an ever-widening gap between the specialist article or monograph, incorporating the results of current research, and general surveys, which inevitably become out of date. *Seminar Studies in History* are designed to bridge this gap. The books are written by experts in their field who are not only familiar with the latest research but have often contributed to it. They are frequently revised, in order to take account of new information and interpretations. They provide a selection of documents to illustrate major themes and provoke discussion, and also a guide to further reading. Their aim is to clarify complex issues without over-simplifying them, and to stimulate readers into deepening their knowledge and understanding of major themes and topics.

ROGER LOCKYER

PREFACE TO THE FIRST EDITION

I would like to acknowledge my great debt to the late Professor Joel Hurstfield whose encouragement was crucial to my development as a historian. Thanks are also due to many of my past students for asking the right questions and to my husband for doing the practical tasks which writers usually seem to leave to their wives: typing, proof-reading and editing.

Finally, I want to thank Roger Lockyer for suggesting the book in the first place and for carefully reading and correcting the first draft.

NOTE ON REFERENCING SYSTEM

Readers should note that numbers in square brackets [5] refer them to the corresponding entry in the Bibliography at the end of the book (specific page numbers are given in italics). A number in square brackets preceded by *Doc.* [*Doc.* 5] refers readers to the corresponding item in the Documents section which follows the main text. Word which are defined in the Glossary are asterisked on their first occurrence in the book.

LIST OF MAPS

ACKNOWLEDGEMENTS

I would like to thank Joanna Coates for reading through and commenting on the typescript.

PART ONE: THE BACKGROUND

1 INTERNATIONAL CONTEXT

For most of the Tudor period Spain and France dominated the European arena, and the rivalry between them was a central feature of international politics. Both states by the 1490s had emerged as strong and powerful after a long period of internal disunity, weak government and partial occupation by foreign powers. In 1479 the Crowns of Aragon and Castile were united in the persons of Ferdinand and Isabella. They reconquered Granada in the south from the Moors in 1492, the same year that Columbus, under their patronage, began the voyage which was to bring Spain an overseas empire. The Spanish monarchs strengthened their position *vis-à-vis* the Spanish nobles, the church and the towns, while creating a centralized authority in their kingdoms, especially Castile. In France a succession of able rulers from Charles VII onwards reasserted royal power and regained lands once conquered or alienated from the Crown. All the territories held by England, save Calais, had been restored to Charles VII by 1453. Picardy, the Somme towns and the ancestral duchy of Burgundy were returned to Louis XI after a series of clashes with his arch-enemy Charles, Duke of Burgundy. The duchy of Brittany was annexed by Charles VIII in 1492. The French kings eroded the privileges of nobles, *pays* and *parlement*, while gaining the effective right of taxing at will.

The focal point of rivalry between these two powers from 1494 to 1559 was Italy. The conflict had small beginnings: the rival dynastic claims of Anjou (Charles VIII) and Aragon to the insignificant and impoverished kingdom of Naples. There were also minor disputes over Cerdagne, Roussillon, Perpignan and Navarre on the Franco-Spanish border. French ambitions in Italy were extended to Milan in 1499 after the accession of Louis XII who had a personal claim to that duchy. The ensuing Italian Wars (1494–1515) ended with the Spanish conquest of Naples and the French capture and then loss of Milan.

A new dimension to Franco-Spanish rivalry arose around the person of Charles V. As duke of Burgundy (1506), king of Spain

(1516), ruler of Austrian Habsburg lands (1516) and Holy Roman Emperor (1519), he impinged on the interests and security of France. First, he ruled over lands which were nominally French fiefs (Artois and Flanders) and which had been coveted by the French kings since the reign of Louis XI. Then, he inherited the disputes over Naples and the territories along the Pyrenees. Furthermore, Milan was an Imperial fief* and more importantly the vital bridge from Charles's territories in the Netherlands, Germany and Franche-Comté to Naples. Finally, France was virtually encircled by Habsburg lands; her borders were vulnerable to Spanish troops (Artois and Flanders were but 290 kilometres from Paris) while any move to expand eastwards would be blocked by a strong hostile power. Dynastic and strategic considerations thus combined to create an intense Habsburg-Valois rivalry to be fought out in a series of wars from 1515 to 1559.

Exhaustion of resources, not the cessation of differences, brought about the end of the wars in the 1559 Treaty of Câteau-Cambrésis. Consequently, Franco-Spanish hostility continued, but as a latent feature of the second half of the sixteenth century. It was latent, not open, because of the French civil wars (1562–98). The collapse of the French monarchy's power in the face of doctrinal strife and aristocratic rebellion prevented France from renewing the wars or even from exploiting effectively Spain's own weaknesses; for Spain too had major problems. The Netherlands were in rebellion in 1566 and again from 1572. At times, the French tried to aid the rebels for their own ends – Coligny in 1571 and Alençon from 1576 till his death in 1584 – but their help was mainly ineffectual. It was Philip II of Spain who broke the uneasy peace when he ordered Parma, commander of the Flanders army, to invade France in 1590 to prevent the Huguenot,* Henry of Navarre, from becoming king. Fear of further and greater French aid to the Dutch rebels, as well as religious considerations, prompted his actions. The war which followed marked the recovery of France, as hatred of Spain overrode domestic doctrinal differences. The Treaty of Vervins (1598) ended the war but again this was only temporary. Franco-Spanish rivalry was to dominate the seventeenth century as it had the sixteenth.

This was the context within which English foreign policy had to operate. Franco-Spanish hostility brought some security to England, as did the internal problems of the two states after 1560. As the earl of Sussex expressed it in 1577: 'the troubles of both places when they have been carried jointly have certainly bred our quiet, and so would continue it if they jointly are continued' [158 *p. 346*]. Yet English governments, without the benefit of hindsight, did not know when a peace might be made permanently or internal problems be settled. French support for a pretender, French intrigues in Scotland, French ambitions in Flanders and a Catholic crusade initiated by either France or Spain were spectres to haunt English governments during the Tudor period. Franco-Spanish rivalry also provided some opportunities for England. If she chose to embark on campaigns to win back her French territories, she could be assured of a powerful ally.

2 OVERSEAS TRADE

In the first half of the sixteenth century, the primary export of England was undyed woollen cloth. Most of it was destined for Antwerp where it was exchanged for a variety of foreign goods, including wines, alum, hemp and iron. The Antwerp money market with its banking, credit and insurance facilities was also widely used by Englishmen, and came to be the main source of government loans from 1544 to 1574. The English economy was so dependent on Antwerp that a foreign observer could cynically remark: 'If Englishmen's fathers were hanged in Antwerp's gate, their children would creep betwixt their legs to come into the said town' [83 *p. 9*].

This fundamental economic fact had repercussions on English foreign policy. First, the governments of both England and the Netherlands recognized the importance of the London-Antwerp trade axis and were consequently anxious to keep on good terms with each other. Second, both were prepared to use the trade as a political bargaining counter. Third, as the market became less stable, English governments began to make diplomatic overtures towards other towns and states, and to back traders, explorers, even privateers seeking new markets.

Economic considerations combined with political interests in encouraging English rulers to maintain friendly relations with the rulers of the Netherlands during the first three-quarters of the Tudor period. Yet whenever serious political differences arose between the two governments, each would sacrifice, or rather use as a weapon, economic interests to obtain political advantages. Henry VII diverted English cloth exports from the Netherlands on two occasions as retaliation for Burgundian protection of his Yorkist enemies; the first in September 1493 and the second in 1505. In 1527 Henry VIII and Wolsey tried to employ similar tactics against Charles V but by then the policy was no longer practicable; not only did customs revenues fall dramatically but unemployment in the cloth industry posed a serious threat to public order. As a result the king was forced to climb down and conclude a truce. During Elizabeth's reign it was the Netherlands' government that initiated economic sanctions. In November 1563 the duchess of Parma (governor of the Netherlands) took advantage of an outbreak of plague in England to place a ban on English imports. She was irritated by English support for heretics in her territories, and indignant at the new export duties which had been introduced in the 1558 Book of Rates. The stoppage, she believed, would force Elizabeth to make concessions. On this occasion, however, the embargo affected Antwerp at least as adversely as it did England, and consequently both governments agreed to resume trade on 1 January 1565. But in December 1568 trade was again suspended, this time for four years, as retaliation against Elizabeth's seizure of Spanish treasure ships [82; 148].

These kinds of political dislocations revealed England's vulnerability in being so heavily reliant on the Antwerp market [*Doc. 1*]. The economic slump of 1551–2 equally demonstrated the dangers of England's dependence on one outlet for its goods. In the second half of the century, therefore, the Merchant Adventurers* were forced to invest in voyagers seeking new markets and trade routes. Moreover, when the political conditions seemed right, they were able to attract government patronage.

Even before this development, Henry VII had attempted to encourage commercial expansion and diversity. Not only did he work to strengthen England's trading position in the Netherlands by negotiating the *Intercursus Magnus* (1496) and *Intercursus Malus* (1506); at the same time he used diplomacy to diversify into other markets and his patronage to encourage the discovery of new trade routes. In 1489 and 1490 he negotiated an agreement with Denmark aimed at extending English trade in the Baltic. The 1378 commercial treaty with Portugal was renewed in 1489; a new Anglo-French commercial treaty was signed in 1497. There were also a treaty with Florence (1490), commercial clauses in treaties with Spain (1489 and 1499) and an abortive treaty with Riga (1499). Henry became patron of first, John Cabot and then his son, Sebastian, in their search for new lands to the west, although admittedly he was not as generous to them as has sometimes been assumed [19; 55]. In effect, Henry's efforts paid low dividends; comparatively few English traders were prepared to forsake the security of the Antwerp market for more risky ventures elsewhere and the royal initiative was not continued under his son.

Only after the 1551 collapse of the Antwerp cloth market did attitudes change. The duke of Northumberland listened to projects of oceanic exploration, and acted as the patron of the French pilot Jean Ribault, Sebastian Cabot and John Dee. With the duke's active support, a joint stock company was established which raised money to finance Sir Hugh Willoughby's and Richard Chancellor's expedition in search of the North-East passage to China and the Indies. The Edwardian Privy Council also promoted attempts to open trade with Morocco and Guinea. Not all of these commercial activities, however, continued to receive royal support under Mary, because the queen's husband, Philip of Spain, wanted to prevent any intrusion by English seamen and traders into the Iberian empires. Consequently, he not only prohibited direct English contacts with Spanish America but also tried to stop the development of trade with Portuguese West Africa. In 1553, in response to Portuguese complaints about the English breaking into their monopoly in Guinea, Philip ordered the Spanish ambassador in England to stop a proposed English voyage to the West African coast [*Doc. 2a*]. Towards the end of 1555, Philip again protested about English encroachments into the Portuguese Empire, and Mary officially halted the Guinea trade [20]. On the other hand, trade with Russia raised no such divided loyalties from Philip. As a result, Mary's government was free to build upon Chancellor's unexpected success in opening up a trade link with Moscow, by assisting in the formation of the Muscovy Company in 1555 and penning a letter to Tsar Ivan IV which elicited a favourable response in the form of a charter of privileges [103]. Philip also invited the explorer, Stephen Borough (who had unsuccessfully made an attempt to find the North-East passage), to visit Seville and allowed him to consult the charts, notebooks and treatises deposited there [55].

A more decisive impulse was provided for commercial expansion and diversification during Elizabeth's reign. After 1564, both political disturbances in the Netherlands and temporary govern-mental embargoes disrupted the Antwerp market and necessitated the finding of alternative outlets in north-west Europe. Briefly during the 1564 crisis, Emden in East Friesland, which was just outside Spanish jurisdiction, was used as a cloth staple.* Then in 1567, nervous about the civil unrest which had rocked the Netherlands the previous year, the Merchant Adventurers backed by the Crown made an agreement with Hamburg which allowed the city to serve as an English cloth staple for ten years. The Adventurers, however, saw this commercial treaty primarily as an insurance measure in the event of further political unrest, and most of the company intended to continue their normal trade with

Antwerp. With the more serious Anglo-Netherlands trade rupture of 1569, however, the London merchants, encouraged by the Privy Council, flocked to the German Lutheran city. Even after the lifting of the embargo in 1573 and signing of the Anglo-Spanish Treaty of Bristol in August 1574, English merchants continued to use Hamburg as their chief continental market, since Calvinist privateers* and rebels operating from their base at Flushing were attacking all shipping which sailed down the River Scheldt towards Antwerp. In the uncertain political and military climate, there was little incentive for the Adventurers to return to their traditional staple. Even before the sack of Antwerp by mutinying Spanish troops in 1576, probably fewer than a score of them were active within the city; thereafter, trade declined still further, 'waxing daily less and less', until English merchants finally departed from the city in 1582 [82 *p. 189*]. Eventually the merchants settled at Emden again (1578–87), Stade (1587–98 and 1601–11) and Middleburg (1587–1621) The government consulted with the merchants in the choice of these towns and gave the trade its support whenever it could [58; 82; 148; 149].

The disruptions caused by the Netherlands Revolt also stimulated commercial ventures by English merchants in the Mediterranean and Baltic [119; 120; 149]. During the 1570s when Philip II employed economic warfare against the Dutch, English merchants filled 'the commercial void and took over the lucrative carrying trade between Northern Europe and the Iberian Peninsula. At the same time merchants started to trade directly with more distant markets where they might not only sell cloth but also purchase luxury items in demand at home. Elizabeth's government gave diplomatic support to many of these activities. The queen repeatedly sent special envoys to Ivan IV to protect and extend the privileges of the Muscovy Company; she also supported the initiative of English merchants, seeking to open up trade with Turkey, by incorporating the Turkey Company in 1581 (the precursor of the Levant Company formed in 1592) [19]. Still more adventurous traders tried to break through the Iberian monopolies in Africa and the Americas. Here Elizabeth was more circumspect in her patronage. She usually left the financial initiative to others and always treated this kind of trade as secondary to European power politics, but for the most part she defended her 'sea-dogs' Hawkins, Drake, Gilbert, Frobisher and Raleigh, when their voyages provoked howls of protest from the Spaniards and Portuguese [19; 102].

By the end of the Tudor period the pattern of overseas trade had changed. 'New markets had been found, new companies incorporated to exploit them, new varieties of cloth produced to sell in them' [83 *p. 82*]. Although Tudor monarchs consistently subordinated economic considerations to political ones of dynasty or defence, nevertheless Henry VII and Elizabeth did much to encourage this extension and diversification of English trade. Their encouragement of foreign trade was designed to consolidate and extend royal power. Both monarchs realized that a flourishing overseas trade meant a high income from the customs and an increase in private shipbuilding which would in turn improve England's naval power. They recognized too the importance of retaining the favour of London merchants who were the source of much-needed crown loans. Finally, they appreciated that commercial expansion would not only enhance royal revenues but also create the impression of power and glory.

3 MILITARY RESOURCES

England's military force under the Tudors was neither as well trained nor as well equipped as those on the Continent. Although there were some seasoned veterans within the ranks, the majority of soldiers were usually inexperienced in warfare. Moreover, their weapons were out of date; lacking firearms and heavy horse, they relied too heavily on the bills and bows which had helped Henry V win at Agincourt a century before. Thus in the French campaign of 1544 barely one-tenth of the 28,000 infantrymen in the army had modern weapons, while apart from fifty Gentlemen Pensioners, there were singularly few men-at-arms [67].

In size, the English armies could bear comparison with the forces of Spain and France, at least during the early Tudor period. The 35,000-strong army which Henry VIII put into the field in 1513 matched in size any of those then fighting in Italy. European armies, however, were to become larger still as the sixteenth century progressed [72; 74]. To try to keep pace imposed an enormous strain on England's resources of men, money and equipment. England's population was at most half that of Spain and a third that of France. The income of the English monarch was far below that of his European counterparts. To make matters even worse, the traditional means of recruiting armies for campaigns overseas was breaking down.

Early Tudor forces, like their medieval predecessors, were recruited in two ways and for two distinct functions. A national militia of able-bodied men was levied in the shires for the purposes of home defence against domestic rebellion and foreign invasion. A contract army was raised by nobles and gentlemen from their household servants, tenants and personal retainers mainly but not exclusively for overseas expeditions. This contract army had always been potentially dangerous to the monarch, as it placed military power in the hands of the nobility, but the first two Tudors were able to place effective controls on noble retinues and harness them to the interests of the Crown. Nonetheless by the 1540s it was becoming very difficult to raise large armies by this means, as landowners were often unco-operative about mustering their retinues. Part of the problem may have been a natural resentment at providing troops for seemingly endless warfare; however, Dr Goring has convincingly suggested that the problem went deeper than this [132]. He argues that the changing composition of the landowning class (due to the dissolution of the monasteries and the disappearance of some noble families) meant that the Crown was obliged to rely on a much wider group of landowners for raising troops. Some of these were obscure country gentlemen whose military resources were difficult for the government to assess accurately. Many of them were forced by inflation to reduce the size of their households and were therefore unable to provide large bands of retainers for the Crown. Whatever the cause, the government found that it needed to turn to another source to supplement the troops levied from landowners' retinues.

The national militia was at hand and from 1544 took on some responsibility for recruiting men to be sent abroad. In this way, and with the additional hire of foreign mercenaries, some 40,000 soldiers were able to participate in the sieges of Boulogne and Montreuil in 1544 while 12,000 men were in Scotland [102; 132]. There were, however, major weaknesses in using both systems for the same purpose. First, the national militia levied a force which was ill-equipped, wholly untrained and poorly organized. This was finally brought home to the government in January 1558 when, after severe problems in actually raising men in the counties for the relief of Calais, fewer than 200 of the 1,000 assembled at Dover were found to have the proper equipment, and this was by no means unique [124]. Secondly, recruiting men by two different but overlapping systems created administrative chaos. Once again it was the Calais campaign which fully exposed the problem. Sometimes commissioners for musters discovered that men on their lists had already been raised by private landowners for their own armies; sometimes they were hampered by landlords trying to keep back their tenants from service so that they might use them in their own bands at some later, and as yet unspecified, date [124].

The Calais débâcle stimulated Mary's 1558 parliament to introduce some reform of the muster system and the law for providing equipment; but it was left to the next reign to build on this foundation and overhaul the military machine. Under Elizabeth, the system was reformed in two major ways: first, a more effective command structure was developed in the counties under lord lieutenants; secondly, from the 1570s onwards regular training of the militia was carried out. In practice a unitary military organization was developed. Although the Crown still used the landowners' retinues as the best means to raise cavalry (for example, Leicester summoned his servants and dependants when embarking on the Netherlands campaign), it relied essentially on its bands of part-time, trained, well-armed militia men for its forces [102; 124; 132]. In the emergency of 1588, the muster system appears to have operated effectively in raising troops quickly for defence against invasion. Just over a week after the first signal beacon had been lit on Cape Lizard at the sighting of the Armada, some 16,000 men were gathering around Lord Hunsdon, the queen's commander in London, and another 12,449 were deployed with the earl of Leicester at Tilbury [145]. In addition, there was a pool of 200,000 militia men available for overseas service in the 1580s, but they were from the poorest social classes, and consequently ill-nourished, badly equipped and largely untrained [32]. Such forces could not compete with the hardened troops of Spain. An important constraint on Elizabeth's foreign policy was her appreciation of the limitations of her army.

The navy, in contrast, grew in size and improved in standard during the Tudor period. Although Henry VII inherited about seven royal ships in 1485 yet passed on only five to his son, he built, in fact, five new ships and captured one. He also stimulated private shipbuilding by offering a royal bounty to subjects who built ships of over 80 tons and by encouraging trade through his so-called Navigation Acts of 1486 and 1489. In addition, his ships were more heavily armed than those of previous reigns, for Henry employed foreign gunners and encouraged the manufacture of ordnance. Armaments were stored at Greenwich and Woolwich and a royal navy dry dock was completed at Portsmouth in 1497. Henry also handed on to his son a more active and firmly-based naval administration based at Portsmouth. Yet despite these important improvements, Henry VII's naval vision was limited; he introduced no major innovations, and it is improbable that he conceived of a standing navy with a regular peacetime function [55; 103].

Henry VIII's contribution to the navy was more ambitious. The new king was deeply interested in both ships and guns, and saw armed ships as his own personal 'status symbol' [55; 89]. During the reign, therefore, he ordered the construction of 46 new ships and bought 26; a further 13 were taken as prizes. He also set up a foundry at Hounsditch where new types and calibres of guns were developed. The firepower of his ships was much greater, as guns began to be placed in the waists of ships to be fired through gun ports at long range. Dockyards were built at Woolwich and Deptford, and Portsmouth was enlarged. A Navy Board was established in 1546, with responsibility for all naval administration. Experienced and able men became in turn its chief working officer, the Treasurer of the Navy, and provided much of the impetus for new designs in shipping. By Henry's death, the royal navy comprised fifty-three serviceable royal ships, twenty-eight of which were over 100 tons. For the first time, these acted as a standing force; during peacetime they were used to suppress piracy or to transport merchants to the Netherlands or Denmark; during periods of naval war, the royal ships did most of the fighting. Additional ships still had to be hired but they constituted no more than half the total fleet and operated only as auxiliaries [55].

Peace with France in 1550 and the pressure for economies temporarily halted the expansion of the navy. Nonetheless some historians are beginning to question whether it suffered from any serious neglect between 1550 and 1555. Professor Loades has pointed out that there was no sudden drop in naval expenditure during these years, but that, on the contrary, spending remained constant at about £20,000 p.a. despite the general demand for retrenchment. The sale of fourteen ships during the early years of Mary's reign, he claims, was not a form of asset-stripping but rather a measure of good housekeeping, as the vessels sold were either old or damaged [55]. Loades therefore disagrees with the view of Tom Glasgow that it was Mary's marriage to Philip II that saved the navy from permanent decline [130]. Although Loades accepts that Philip showed a keen interest in England's naval capacity, he can detect no change in naval policy after the king's arrival in England nor any new programme of shipbuilding and repair before the outbreak of war. Both historians would agree, however, that the French War resulted in a resumption of ship construction (the completion of three new ships and the commencement of four more) and saw an effective use of sea power [55; 131].

During the reign of Elizabeth royal shipbuilding continued apace: there were 25 warships of various sizes constructed between 1558 and 1588 [55]. Unlike her father, however, Elizabeth relied heavily on private English shipping for her fleets. Of the 197 ships in service against the Spaniards between March and August 1588, almost half were provided by private shipowners. A year later only eight ships out of the fleet of one hundred and fifty which set sail for Portugal belonged to the queen. Elizabeth put up nearly half the capital for the expedition, but privateers provided the actual ships in the hope of profit from plunder [16]. At the same time Elizabeth lent her ships and equipment for private commercial enterprises in return for a share of the profits. From 1564, the queen and many of her councillors invested in and supported the privateering expeditions of captains like Hawkins and Drake [20; 55] [*Doc. 2b*]. Both private and royal ships improved in design and in fighting power, especially after the 1570s. The royal warship, the *Revenge*, was the pride of its day but not unique in its ability to sink ships at long range and voyage across the oceans [19; 30; 55; 102]. On the other hand the naval administration under Elizabeth stagnated. It was manned by a narrow interest group, often connected by blood or marriage. who held their positions for a remarkable length of time; Benjamin Gonson, for example, held his office as Treasurer for twenty years from 1549 until his death in 1578, when he was succeeded by his son-in-law, John Hawkins. The administration also became a prey to corruption [55; 108].

The idea of the sea as a protective, though not complete, moat around England predated the Tudors. The loss of their lands in France, however, and the expansion of France into the Channel ports of Brittany and Picardy, brought home to Tudor Englishmen their vulnerability to attack and the need for a navy as a first line of defence [97]. Under Henry VII no naval strategy had been developed and the navy was rarely used for offensive engagements. Then, during the French wars of 1543–46 privateering in the Channel became common, sanctioned by letters of marque* issued by the government. It was soon realized that great profits could be gained from such ventures for government and privateers alike. The navy thus became transformed in two ways in the sixteenth century. From a coastal defence force, auxiliary to the army, it became an ocean-going, aggressive, striking power. From a small fleet which was reinforced in wartime by the hire of (usually foreign) vessels, the English navy became large but comprised royal and private shipping. Thus, whereas royal control over the army was virtually complete, over the navy it was weak. In consequence, though well armed, modern in design and a match for the Spaniards, the navy suffered from 'divergent aims and disunited commands' [102 *p. 135*].

An active foreign policy required money as well as men. Munitions, fortifications, the wages of mercenaries, all had to be paid for; and war was becoming an increasingly expensive business in the inflationary sixteenth century. The English monarchs simply did not have the ordinary resources to finance lengthy wars. Their ordinary revenues have been estimated at £100,000–£150,000 which barely covered ordinary expenditure. Parliamentary taxation had to be levied but was inadequate for wartime needs, since parliament was growing increasingly unwilling to finance military campaigns. By Edward VI's reign parliament only contributed some 22 per cent of the total military spending [38]. At times of war, therefore, governments had to resort to expedients such as forced loans, sales of Crown lands, debasements of the currency and the sale of monopolies.

War finance could bear hard on the country and was sometimes resisted by taxpayers. Tax rebellions thwarted the war policy of Henry VII in 1489 and 1497, while refusal to pay Henry VIII's Amicable Grant in 1525 sank his plans for an invasion of France. By contrast, in the 1540s, Henry was remarkably successful in demanding and exacting enormous parliamentary levies. Here 'the triumph of Henry's will' was facilitated by a run of good harvests (with the exception of 1545), visible military achievements and the sense of national emergency in 1545, when the French fleet sailed up the Solent [38 *p. 138*]. Moreover, Henry's ministers took account of potential popular dissatisfaction with war finance and fixed forced loans at lower rates than those of the 1520s. Edward's government continued to make heavy tax demands but dared not request forced loans. Mary faced some difficulty in raising a war subsidy in 1558 and had to resort to forced loans but she levied them cautiously [38]. After 1585, Elizabeth and her ministers were understandably unwilling to impose heavy financial burdens on the realm for fear of 'a general murmur of the people'. Partly for this reason, the queen was prepared to make stringent economies and sell off her assets to share the responsibility of meeting the costs of war. Nonetheless, during the 1590s, taxpayers faced an annual demand of about £90,000 in contrast with the £33,000 a year average payment in the 1570s, and by the end of the reign there were many signs of war-weariness coming from the localities [151 *p. 25*; 61].

4 THE MAKING OF FOREIGN POLICY

Foreign policy was the prerogative of monarchs. They could ask advice from councillors but were in no way bound by it [*Doc. 3*]. Nevertheless, rarely were major foreign policy decisions taken without monarchs consulting the Privy Council or individual councillors informally. The principal secretary (especially Thomas Cromwell, Francis Walsingham and William and Robert Cecil) had the most obvious influence on day-to-day policy decisions. They tended to choose diplomatic envoys, usually drafted their instructions, and routinely processed despatches sent to and from foreign posts [36; 94; 114; 148]. Conflicting conciliar views were frequently received on matters large and small, but while to some extent this gave monarchs freedom of action, they were usually cautious about pursuing ambitious policies without first winning over a substantial group of councillors. Thus, Mary did not yield to her husband's pleas that England should join Spain in its war against France until Stafford's raid had convinced the 'doves' in the Council of the inevitability of England's participation in the war. Similarly, Elizabeth felt unable to marry the duke of Anjou in 1579 because of the opposition from most of her councillors.

Parliament officially had no role to play in the making of foreign policy, although its power to vote or deny taxation might act as a restraining hand on a monarch who planned war. Yet parliament rarely resisted taxation; indeed it was rather the unwillingness of the country to pay taxes, sometimes already granted by parliament, that led the monarch on occasion to rethink his policies. The Cornish rebels in 1497, who protested against paying for the king's Scottish war, forced Henry VII to make a peace. Local resistance to the unparliamentary 'Amicable Grant' in 1525 effectively sabotaged Henry VIII's plans for another invasion of France. Although these cases were exceptional, they were important in demonstrating the limitations of royal power to the monarchs themselves. When Elizabeth finally resorted to war against Spain, she showed a greater reluctance than her father to squeeze the country financially, perhaps because she feared popular insurrections [102; 103]. Elizabeth's respect for public opinion manifested itself in another significant way. From 1576 onwards, she allowed her privy councillors to place before parliament explanations of her policy in order to win parliamentary support and subsidies. Sir Walter Mildmay or Sir Christopher Hatton presented national security problems and an exposition of the government's policies to the Commons in 1576, 1581, 1584, 1585 and 1587. As Professor MacCaffrey has written, their speeches transformed foreign policy 'from an arcane preserve of the Crown into a topic of wide public concern' [60 *p. 485*]. In 1587, however, the councillors clearly exceeded their instructions, when they tried to use parliament to put pressure on the queen to accept the sovereignty of the Netherlands. Elizabeth had already rejected such an idea in Council and the councillors who favoured a forward policy in the Netherlands were trying to force the queen to change her mind. Although the attempt failed, it 'casts a great deal of light on the winding intricacies of Elizabethan policy making' [60 *p. 490*].

Two further points need to be made about the formulation of foreign policy. The first concerns the nature of the diplomatic service and the role of ambassadors in policy-making. In general terms, the Tudor period saw a growth in diplomatic personnel and a greater bureaucratization of the administration [23; 43; 65; 121; 157]. Nonetheless, there were very few permanent English representatives at foreign courts, and the monarch usually had to rely on informal agents to supply information and temporary ambassadors for specific diplomatic missions. The quality of all these men varied enormously; some were competent linguists and experienced negotiators while others were simply not up to the job.

For most of Henry VIII's reign, diplomats were not careerist government servants but rather soldiers and courtiers whose status at a foreign court depended on the intimacy they enjoyed with their royal master. The number of clerics employed on diplomatic missions was also relatively high (certainly in comparison with the clerical envoys used by Francis I). By the 1540s, however, some experienced envoys (for example Bishop Gardiner and William Paget) had been promoted to powerful positions at home because of their successful performance abroad and were being viewed by Henry as experts in foreign affairs [163; 147]. During Elizabeth's reign, it seems that 'a subtle revolution' took place and that for the first time there emerged career diplomats who functioned as specialists in particular geographical regions. The government not only depended on these men as sources of information but relied upon their judgement and advice both when they were on assignments abroad and occupied in royal service at home. Daniel Rogers and Dr John Herbert, for example, were employed repeatedly on Elizabethan missions to northern Germany and the Baltic, and also acted as 'the main sources of information and expertise for this area' during their time at court. Similarly, Sir Thomas Wilkes, Sir Thomas Bodley and Sir William Davison were sent frequently as envoys to the Netherlands and were 'always consulted at home' about events in the Low Countries [114 *pp. 276–7*]. But men who helped form policy in this way were not neutral observers of the international scene. Many of them had their own religious and political agendas, ones which they usually shared with their patrons on the Council. Thus during the 1570s and 1580s an increasing number of representatives abroad promoted the policy of international interventionism which was favoured by Leicester and Walsingham [60; 114].

The second point of interest is the influence which merchants and those investing in trade had on policy. More work still needs to be carried out in this area, but even at the present state of research the merchant interest appears to be a steady, though by no means monolithic, pressure group. Under Henry VII London merchants encouraged the king to improve relations with the Burgundian court. Under Elizabeth, those involved in Iberian trade tried to encourage harmonious relations with Spain, while those investing in privateering did not flinch from confrontation or conflict with Spain. For example, Iberian merchants pressed the government to restore Drake's spoils in 1580 to avoid a breach with Spain, whereas investors and sponsors of his voyage urged the government to keep the treasure [19]. During the Spanish War, merchants suggested military strategies which reflected their economic interests, as when in 1589 a group of London merchants, among them leading promoters of privateering, put a scheme to the Privy Council for an exploratory three-ship voyage to India and the East Indies [99].

The making of foreign policy was thus a complex and intricate business. It was done on the basis of inadequate knowledge of European affairs and often in the face of conflicting advice. But for the historian one of the most difficult, if not insoluble, problems is to determine to what extent monarch or minister made policy. Was it Wolsey or Henry VIII, Cromwell or Henry VIII, Burghley or Elizabeth? The following analysis should help to provide some answers.

PART TWO: ANALYSIS

5 HENRY VII 1485–1509

INTRODUCTION

Henry VII's foreign policy is at last in the process of re-evaluation. Until recently, his foreign policy was conventionally described as merely an extension of his domestic policy, his aims in both being to secure his dynasty by quelling plots of pretenders to the throne and by ensuring the succession through his descendants [18; 28; 56; 90; 97]. The traditional royal pursuit of glory and chivalric ideals seemed to have no place in his thinking; instead Henry appeared to be consistently following a policy of peace, mending relations with England's ancient enemies, France and Scotland, and remaining detached from new international conflicts focused on Italy. Nowadays, however, historians are rethinking this analysis. Their researches suggest that the pacifist element in his foreign policy has been overrated and that his unwillingness to spend money on military preparations or on promoting his royal image abroad has been greatly exaggerated [21; 111; 112; 121; 122; 128]. The following analysis reflects this new approach.

POLICY OF PEACE?

From the moment of his accession, Henry initiated alliances with other European princes. A one-year truce with France was proclaimed in October 1485 and was soon extended to last until January 1489. In 1486 Henry signed a three-year truce with Scotland and tried unsuccessfully to arrange a marriage alliance between the two realms. In the same year a commercial treaty was made with the duke of Brittany. Henry began negotiations for a marriage between his son, Arthur, and Catherine of Aragon in 1488, which was agreed in the Treaty of Medina del Campo the next year [Doc. 4] [28]. There can be little doubt that the main impetus behind these alliances and treaties was dynastic security. Hostile courts abroad might provide a haven for Yorkist pretenders to the throne, whereas friendly rulers would recognize Henry's legitimacy, thus improving his credibility at home.

It soon became evident, however, that these treaties were not an effective barrier against foreign aid for Yorkist pretenders. Duchess Margaret of Burgundy (Edward IV's sister and step-mother-in-law of the Austrian Archduke, Maximilian) consistently gave practical and diplomatic help to any challenge to Henry VII's rule [96]. In 1491 Charles VIII of France was organizing a Yorkist rebellion. Between late 1495 and the summer of 1497, James IV of Scotland gave refuge to Perkin Warbeck, who was impersonating Edward IV's younger son, Richard Duke of York. He even arranged for the pretender to marry his cousin, Lady Catherine Gordon [21; 71; 96; 128]. Apart from Duchess Margaret, who hated the usurper, Henry Tudor, these influential supporters of Warbeck used him merely as a pawn in diplomacy. They only gave him aid when they were antagonistic to Henry and hoped either to force the English king to follow their will or to replace him with a more pliable figure. They were, therefore, quite prepared to abandon Warbeck either in return for diplomatic concessions or, in the case of Henry, proving to be too powerful to offend. Thus Charles VIII honoured Warbeck when he was experiencing difficulties with Henry over his plans to absorb Brittany into France, and James IV helped Warbeck because he wanted the return of the fortress of Berwick held by the English since 1482 [18; 21; 56; 128]. Henry would not, however, submit to this kind of diplomatic pressure. Conscious of his insecure hold on his kingdom, he could not risk his credibility at home by adopting too weak and conciliatory a policy overseas. As a consequence he was forced to use military action or its threat, as well as diplomacy, to resolve these dangers to his dynasty.

Henry's readiness to use the military option can be seen both during the Breton Crisis of 1489–92 and in his preparations for war against Scotland during 1496–7. In the former case the king was prepared to raise an army to protect the autonomous duchy of Brittany from annexation by the French Crown. Henry realized that were the duchy to be absorbed into France, England would lose a potential ally in any future conflict with the French king. Furthermore, he understood that the French acquisition of the Breton coastline would endanger the realm's security; from its maritime bases an invasion of England could be launched or English merchant-shipping, trading with Spain and Gascony, could be attacked [*Doc. 5*]. Consequently, when the French planned to marry the young Duchess Anne of Brittany to Charles VIII, Henry decided on intervention. Initially, he tried to limit the extent of his military commitment, because his resources were limited and his hold on the throne still tenuous. By the Treaty of Redon (14 February 1489) he agreed to send a small force of 6,000 men for the duchy's defence on the condition that the Bretons paid their expenses. In addition, in order to share the burden of providing aid, Henry made alliances with Maximilian of Austria and Ferdinand of Aragon [18; 97]. Nonetheless, in 1489 he asked parliament for a directly assessed and renewable subsidy of £75,000 to pay for a war in Brittany. The tax, however, proved difficult to collect and provoked a rising in Yorkshire. Henry was also let down by his allies; Spain had sent some 2,000 men in 1490 but soon recalled them to participate in the conquest of Granada, and Maximilian was preoccupied with his family's dynastic claims to Hungary.

Henry's small-scale expedition to Brittany was consequently a failure. In December 1491, Charles captured Rennes and married Duchess Anne. Britanny had effectively become part of France. To make matters worse, Charles demonstrated his anger at Henry VII's intervention by dispatching an envoy to Ireland to fetch Perkin Warbeck to his court. The danger from the French at this point seemed so great that Henry began preparing for war. A search through the records has revealed that the king sealed numerous indentures with his knights and retainers for levying an army, and issued commissions for purveying supplies and mustering craftsmen and labourers for the army. His plan was to invade France in early June 1492 with the help of Maximilian and to send troops to Brittany where his agent was plotting with Breton leaders to arrange the surrender of Brest and Morlaix. Accordingly, Henry asserted his claim to the French throne and persuaded parliament to vote him additional revenues for war. As the late spring and summer advanced, however, it became clear that Maximilian would not meet his military commitments and that the French had organized their defences too well for an assault on Normandy or Brittany. In these circumstances, Henry had to abandon his scheme and salvage his honour as best he could [122]. In October 1492, when the campaigning season was nearly over, he landed with an army of 26,000 men at Calais and a few weeks later he began to besiege Boulogne, all the while keeping up negotiations with the French. This military episode is correctly described as an act of bravado and no more than 'bargaining chips' designed to improve Henry's negotiating position with Charles VIII [31; 71]. Nonetheless, it should not be forgotten that in early 1492 Henry had been planning a war, not just a demonstration of strength.

Charles, anxious to be free to pursue adventures in Italy, quickly offered peace-terms which Henry equally swiftly accepted. On 3 November 1492, the two kings concluded the Treaty of Étaples, whereby Henry agreed to withdraw from France (with the exception of Calais) and abandon his claim to the French throne, while Charles promised to pay an indemnity of about £159,000 in half-yearly instalments of £2,000 and to refuse aid to Yorkist or other rebels.

Henry VII showed an equal readiness to prosecute war after James IV of Scotland raided England in September 1496 as the ally of Perkin Warbeck. Although the raid itself was small-scale and failed in its objective of fomenting rebellion in the north, it once more demonstrated to Henry that James IV was prepared to lend his prestige to Warbeck's pretensions. Consequently, Henry responded by declaring war on Scotland, and throughout the winter of 1496–7 he made careful preparations for a major offensive: agents were sent to Flanders for the purpose of hiring well-armed mercenary troops, ordinances were issued to organize the supply of the newest weaponry and ordnance; to pay for the venture he requested a grant of £120,000 from his 1497 parliament and secured loans of over £51,000. It has been estimated that, by June 1497, at least £60,000 had been spent and possibly as much as £90,000. Henry was aiming at a knock-out blow against the Scots. An army of 20,000 men was to be sent across the borders while seventy ships containing 5,000 men were to attack Aberdeen and Edinburgh [111; 128].

It was the 1497 Cornish rebellion that effectively put paid to Henry's plans for war and led him to open diplomatic negotiations with James IV in July. James, seriously alarmed at the prospect of an English invasion, was willing to accept almost any terms for peace and quickly agreed to the expulsion of Warbeck from his kingdom in the seven-year Truce of Ayton signed on the 30 September 1497. The loss of this last courtly haven brought about the end of the Warbeck threat, and after a feeble attempt to stir a Yorkist rising in Ireland and Cornwall, the pretender surrendered to Henry.

For the remainder of the reign, maintenance of good relations with Scotland and France was central to Henry's foreign policy. The 'Auld Alliance' between these two realms could have no force if one or both of them were allied to England. In this policy Henry was entirely successful. The Truce of Ayton was followed by a full-blown peace-treaty in 1502 and a dynastic marriage between James IV and Henry's elder daughter, Margaret Tudor, in 1503.

Similarly the rapprochement with France at Étaples was easily retained. When Henry joined the Holy League, which was initially formed to combat French conquests in Italy, he made it clear that he had no intention of fighting against France, and the next year (1497) he signed a commercial treaty with Charles VIII. On the death of Charles in 1498, Henry refused to countenance the suggestion of Maximilian that they should launch a joint invasion against Louis XII. Similarly, he would not agree to attack France when asked to do so by Ferdinand of Aragon in 1502. Although Henry always feared French expansionism in Flanders as a potential danger to England, French ambitions under Charles VIII and Louis XII lay elsewhere and their campaigns in Italy comprised no threat to English interests.

At the same time, Henry was able to continue his alliance with Spain until the last years of the reign. The Treaty of Medina del Campo was followed a decade later by a marriage alliance between Henry's heir, Arthur, and Catherine of Aragon. In October 1501, the couple were married in England. The Spanish alliance not only brought Henry the friendship of the most important power in Europe but also that of the Netherlands, since the heiress to Spain, Joanna, was married to Maximilian's son, Archduke Philip of Burgundy. Thus when Arthur died in April 1502 Henry was no less anxious than the Spanish monarchs were that the marriage alliance should be preserved. Within six months an English treaty was drafted to arrange a marriage between the widowed Catherine and the new heir, Prince Henry. A formal treaty was signed in June 1503 but it decreed that the marriage should not take place until Prince Henry reached the age of fourteen [28].

Thus from 1494 until 1504, at a time when the peace of Western Europe was shattered by the Italian Wars, Henry was able to remain on good terms with each of the main participants. They all sought his friendship in the hope that he might be induced to enter the wars on their side. Throughout his reign Henry had made great efforts to enhance his reputation at home and abroad, spending considerable sums on ostentatious displays of wealth and power: constructing warships which displayed the royal banners, lavishly entertaining foreign envoys, putting on splendid chivalric spectacles, and employing Burgundian artists to decorate his palaces and paint royal portraits [37; 55; 121]. For this reason, reports exaggerating his revenues and military potential circulated European courts and made him appear a desirable ally [Doc. 6].

THREATS TO THE DYNASTY FROM BURGUNDY

Henry's dynastic insecurities had an important effect on foreign policy. As already seen, it nearly drew him into military confrontation with France in 1492 and Scotland in 1496. In addition it adversely affected England's relationship with its traditional ally, the Burgundian rulers of the Netherlands, for the dowager Duchess Margaret, Maximilian of Austria, and Philip of Burgundy repeatedly offered a base to Henry's political opponents and rivals. The earliest plots – the Staffords' rising of 1486 and Lambert Simnel's imposture of 1487 – were not too serious; but the latter did indicate the problem of foreign support for conspiracies, as Margaret had provided 2,000 German mercenaries for the venture. Nevertheless Henry was able to suppress these risings without having to take action against Margaret [24].

Perkin Warbeck's activities, however, were more dangerous. After his expulsion from France in 1492, Margaret welcomed him in Flanders and publicly recognized him as her nephew. Maximilian, angry with Henry for having concluded a separate peace with France, ignored English diplomatic protests and allowed Warbeck a safe haven in his territories. Henry's reaction was both swift and tough. Risking his customs revenues and mercantile discontent, he ordered the suspension of English trade with the Low Countries in September 1493. Maximilian and Margaret, however, proved intransigent and refused to submit to this commercial pressure. Instead, they imposed a counter-embargo and in December 1494 made a formal agreement with Warbeck. Under their protection, the adventurer was able to extend his conspiracy to include James IV, Irish nobles and English Yorkists. Henry's intelligence network, however, soon uncovered the plans, and the king quickly and effectively dealt with the threat. In October 1494 Edward Poynings was dispatched to Ireland to secure it from a Warbeck invasion, while at home a series of treason trials was conducted and several English gentlemen were executed.

In 1495 Maximilian intimated that he would abandon Warbeck if Henry joined the Holy League, but as Henry refused to fight against France, Maximilian stepped up his support and encouraged Warbeck to land in England with a small force. Warbeck's arrival at Deal in Kent in July 1495 was a total fiasco, and the pretender fared no better when he turned his efforts to Ireland. After this, he looked to James IV for aid and hoped for a joint Scottish-Burgundian invasion of England. By this time, however, Maximilian had lost confidence in his protégé. Furthermore, the damage to the Netherlands' trade, alarm about Charles VIII's success in Italy and the initiation of further negotiations to include Henry in the League, all convinced Maximilian that he had more to gain from the friendship of Henry than from that of Perkin Warbeck. Consequently, a commercial treaty was signed in February 1496, known later as the *Intercursus Magnus*, which included the stipulation that each government would not protect the other's rebels and that if Margaret would not follow this directive she would lose her dower lands [18; 71; 97].

The threats to the dynasty, however, did not die with the capitulation of Warbeck in September 1497 after another abortive rising in England. Edmund de la Pole, Earl of Suffolk, and his brother Richard fled from Henry's court in 1501 and persuaded Maximilian to give them support against Henry. The deaths of two of his sons had intensified Henry's sense of dynastic insecurity, for he showed even greater anxiety about the Poles than about Warbeck [18; 50]. It was possibly in reaction to this crisis that Henry persuaded his parliament in 1504 to renew the privileges and rights of the Hanse,* since he remembered that Edward IV had recovered his throne in 1471 by means of Hanseatic support. It was only when Henry secured custody of Suffolk, in 1506, that he reverted to his earlier policy of eroding the Hanse's privileged position [58]. Certainly, the 1505 ban on all cloth destined for the Netherlands was intended to drive Maximilian into surrendering Suffolk. In fact, Suffolk's capture was partly the result of chance. In January 1506 a storm drove the ship of Philip of Burgundy and his wife to take refuge at a harbour in Dorset. Henry, taking advantage of this opportunity, welcomed the two at his court and signed a treaty of alliance with them. In the treaty, Philip promised to give no further aid to Henry's rebels and the following month he handed over Suffolk.

THE LAST YEARS

Henry's foreign policy during the last five or so years of his life had to respond to two major crises; the first threatened his dynasty, while the second endangered the pattern of friendships he had constructed so carefully. The deaths of Henry's two sons, Edmund (1500) and Arthur (1502), and of his wife, Elizabeth (1503), revived fears for the continuity of the Tudor dynasty. Henry now had only one male heir, Prince Henry, a boy of uncertain health and still only eleven years old in 1502. Henry's concern manifested itself in his arrest of two nephews of Edward IV and his ruthless treatment of potential traitors; fifty-one Acts of Attainder passed through the parliament of 1504. Another way of meeting the crisis was to marry and beget another heir. This Henry tried to do when he unsuccessfully sought the hand in turn of Queen Joanna of Naples, niece to Ferdinand of Aragon, Margaret of Savoy, daughter of Emperor Maximilian, and Joanna, widow of Philip of Burgundy who had died in 1506.

The death of Isabella of Castile in 1504 produced the second crisis. Her death ended the dynastic unity of Spain, as her husband Ferdinand, King of Aragon, had neither title nor power in Castile. Only if Joanna, heiress to Castile, allowed her father to act as regent there until his own death, could the unity of the two Crowns be preserved. But Joanna's husband, Philip of Burgundy, insisted that she accept her inheritance immediately. Thus it looked as if Spain might disintegrate and Henry's powerful ally be reduced to a minor princeling. Henry could not afford to wait upon events. Prince Henry was supposed to marry Ferdinand's daughter, Catherine, in 1505, a marriage which was looking more and more like a misalliance. Furthermore, France might take advantage of the situation and possibly reassert its claims to Flanders. Henry's response to the crisis was to draw closer to Maximilian and Philip of Burgundy. Commercial relations between England and Burgundy were of great importance, whereas Anglo-Spanish trade was minimal. Moreover, Philip of Burgundy seemed more likely to win the contest against his father-in-law, who was elderly and unpopular with the Castilian nobility. Finally, Henry's aid to Philip might be rewarded by the Burgundian surrender of the earl of Suffolk which would end the Yorkist conspiracy against his throne.

Therefore, Henry was prepared to abandon the Spanish alliance which had up till then been a key element in his foreign policy. In June 1505 he arranged for Prince Henry to protest against the Spanish match before Bishop Fox, and he openly sought a French or Burgundian bride for his son. At the same time, he advanced huge sums to Philip to finance his expedition to Castile: £138,000 in 1505 alone. It was during this period of close co-operation with Burgundy that Philip and Joanna unexpectedly became Henry's guests in early 1506. The treaty which Henry was able to negotiate with Philip in February offered English support to Joanna and arranged for Henry to marry Philip's sister, Margaret of Savoy; before leaving, Philip agreed to hand over Suffolk and empowered several of his attendants to negotiate a trade alliance which was afterwards dubbed the *Intercursus Malus* by the Flemings because it was so favourable to England,

But shortly after Philip had successfully taken control of Castile for Joanna, he died, and his wife (it was said) went mad with grief. Ferdinand of Aragon was able to regain power in Castile while Margaret of Savoy ruled the Netherlands as regent for her six-year-old nephew, Archduke Charles. Henry's diplomacy was in shreds. Afraid that France might exploit the opportunity to seize land in Flanders, Henry tried to draw closer to Maximilian and repair links with Spain. When Margaret of Savoy at last rejected his marriage proposal in 1508, Henry offered his hand to Joanna. He believed her 'madness' was mere propaganda on the part of Ferdinand who planned to rule in her place, and that Ferdinand would be pleased with the match since Joanna would thereafter be whisked off to England out of his way. Ferdinand, however, now that he was in control of Castile and allied to France, had no need to be reconciled with England. He would neither agree to Joanna's marriage nor send the remainder of the dowry of his daughter, Catherine, to England which would allow her marriage with Prince Henry to go ahead.

For the brief remainder of his life, Henry tried unsuccessfully to isolate Ferdinand. His daughter, Mary, married Maximilian's grandson, Archduke Charles by proxy in 1508. As part of the matrimonial settlement, he was prepared to suspend the commercial concessions he had won for English merchants in the *Intercursus*. Negotiations were afoot for other marriage alliances with France and the Empire, and at one point he even suggested to the French that Prince Henry marry Margaret of Angoulême, sister to the heir presumptive of France. But in December 1508, Spain joined the League of Cambrai against Venice – a league which included France, the Empire and the Papacy but not England [18; 28; 97]. Yet, in fact, there was no cause for alarm, as its members cultivated England's friendship. Furthermore, the alliance seemed to guarantee that France, Spain and the emperor would remain fixated on Italy, where no English interests were at stake.

CONCLUSION

Henry's foreign policy failed in detail; neither the expedition to relieve Brittany, nor the attempts to isolate Ferdinand after 1507 were a success. His policy also proved expensive; between 1505 and 1509 he gave £342,000 in cash, plate or jewels to the Habsburgs

[50]. Yet when Henry died, he left his country and dynasty internationally secure. There was no threat of foreign military intervention in England's internal affairs. Although England was not a member of the League of Cambrai, its members were not hostile to England and were preoccupied with Italy. European rulers respected Henry's power and sought his friendship. Henry's success can be judged by 'comparing the extreme weakness of his international position in 1485 with its unspectacular but substantial strength towards the end of his reign' [28 *p. 273*]. It has been generally recognized that his success was based on the firm foundation of domestic strength and realistic objectives in foreign policy; it is now being suggested that his achievements also 'owe a great deal more to his expertise in warfare than has been fashionable to acknowledge' [111 *p. 1*].

6   HENRY VIII

INTRODUCTION

Henry VIII spent about a quarter of his reign in open war against
France. The earliest campaigns took place between 1512 and 1514;
then in 1522 Henry entered the first of the many Habsburg-Valois
wars between Francis I and Charles V, and he only made peace in
1525 when tax revolts forced his hand. For the next fifteen years
the international politics surrounding Henry's divorce compelled
him to seek a *rapprochement* with the French king. In 1543,
however, Charles V proposed an offensive alliance against France
and as his ally, Henry invaded the Boulonnais. Even after the
emperor had abandoned the campaign in 1544, Henry kept up the
fighting until June 1546 [25; 134].

Henry was not drawn into these wars by bellicose ministers or a
military nobility. He did not provoke wars in order to channel the
energies of his subjects away from private feuds or anti-monarchical
activities. Nor did he fight to defend England's strategic interests.
Brought up in a society where the chivalric ideal still counted,
Henry fought for honour. He was 'not unmindful that it was his
duty to seek fame by military skill' and sought recognition of his
valour and military prowess by success in battle; in this way his
warfare was an extension of the tournaments, of which he was so
fond [11 *p. 161*; 134]. Honour demanded, too, that the king should
assert his rights to the French throne and take back his ancestral
lands, especially Normandy and Guienne. By winning the French
wars Henry hoped to find a place for himself in national history. As
Lord Mountjoy announced: 'Our king does not desire gold or gems
or precious metals, but virtue, glory, immortality' [134 *p. 40*]. Honour
was the ultimate prize, but nonetheless war was never just a game,
simply 'the sport of kings', a dilettante activity. There were always
the dangers of invasion, diplomatic isolation, dynastic challenges
and unfavourable deals in a peace-treaty. Loss of honour could
bring in its wake threats to England's defence and interests.

Moreover, the pursuit of honour did not seem either irresponsible or unrealistic to the king and political nation. Only a few contemporaries had any idea of the long-term economic damage that warfare could inflict, while the human costs in terms of life, limbs or livelihoods were not highly valued. Despite some recognition that England was no longer a great martial nation, the prevailing view of the operation of the wheel of history made it seem possible, even likely, that France's fortunes were due for a fall and therefore Henry could repeat the early victories of the Hundred Years' War [25; 129; 134].

1509-14

From the moment of his accession, Henry VIII was bent on war against France. It was no coincidence that one of his earliest actions was to commission a translation of the life of Henry V, the warrior king whom Henry took as his model. By the end of 1509 he had reinforced Calais, ordered general musters, commissioned new artillery and initiated an expansion programme for the navy [88; 134; 163]. The international scene in 1509, however, did not present the opportunity for immediate war against France. At that time, the French king, Louis XII, was co-operating with the Empire, Spain and most of Italy in Pope Julius II's League of Cambrai against Venice. Henry's first task, therefore, was to effect the isolation of France. With this end in view, he sent Archbishop Bainbridge of York to Rome, both to reconcile the Venetians with the pope and to encourage Julius to enter an alliance which would counter French influence in Italy. The mission was not difficult, as the Venetians had already suffered serious defeats and Julius was beginning to appreciate that the French were the main threat to papal independence. Consequently, Bainbridge was successful in helping to form a league against France in November 1511 and, more importantly, in laying the foundations for a long period of Anglo-papal co-operation [27; 101].

Louis's response to the pope's attempts to create a league against him was to summon a General Council of the Church* to Pisa. This act challenged the power of the pope and thereby played into the hands of Julius, who could present his league as a holy one against a schismatic king. It also helped Henry to unite his Council behind war and, in particular, to overrule the clerical councillors who had argued for a continuation of peace and had been responsible for the renewal of the Treaty of Étaples with France in 1510 [88]. In

November 1511, Henry and Ferdinand of Aragon agreed to mount a joint invasion against France on behalf of the Holy League, and decided to attack and conquer Guienne for Henry. However, while Spanish troops captured Navarre, the soldiers of the English army under Dorset mutinied or died of dysentery. In 1513 Henry tried his luck in Flanders, with Maximilian as his ally, and this campaign gave Henry the glory he craved. Under his leadership the English army won a cavalry skirmish, grandiosely dubbed the Battle of the Spurs, destroyed the French fortress at Thérouanne and occupied Tournai, which was a French enclave in Burgundian territory. During the campaign, his army had captured six standards of France, four of which were extremely prestigious, and sent home at least thirty-one prisoners of high status [163]. 'The victory hath been so great that I think none hath been seen before', wrote Queen Catherine with more enthusiasm than accuracy, for the strategic value of Henry's gains was negligible [33 *p. 118*]. Tournai, granted to England in the 1514 peace, was an expensive outpost, which was to cost twice as much to garrison and fortify as it paid in tribute, while it was the emperor rather than Henry who benefited from the destruction of the French fortress at Thérouanne and the expulsion of the French from Tournai [38; 33].

While Henry was enjoying the taste of war in Flanders, a far more important victory was won against the Scots. Relations between Henry and his brother-in-law, James IV, had deteriorated soon after the renewal of the 1502 Anglo-Scottish treaty at Henry's accession. By 1512 James IV was the ally of France and in the next year he crossed the border and seized Norham Castle in England [137]. Meanwhile Catherine, governor of the realm in Henry's absence, and the earl of Surrey raised 30,000–40,000 men to fight the Scots. There followed a massive defeat for Scotland at Flodden in September 1513 when the Scots lost their king and well over 10,000 men. 'This battle hath been to your grace and all your realm the greatest honour that could be, and more than ye should win the Crown of France, thanken be God for it' wrote Catherine, with more accuracy than tact [33 *p. 118*]. But the victory was not exploited, for instead of sending an English army to occupy Scotland, Henry merely left his sister there as regent for the seventeen-month-old heir, in the hope that she would rule the country in his interests. Scotland was a low priority in Henry's foreign policy; his aim was not to dominate the kingdom but to neutralize it during his wars against France [137].

During the French war, Ferdinand and Maximilian had

manipulated Henry into following a military strategy that suited themselves but was of little advantage to the English king. In 1514 Henry was again to be tricked by his allies. Although both had agreed to campaign with Henry against France before the end of 1514, Ferdinand first, then Maximilian, made separate peace treaties with Louis XII. Consequently, Henry was left to fight alone. As Louis had also come to terms with the new Pope, Leo X, Henry was soon persuaded, though reluctantly, to open negotiations with France. In August 1514 a peace treaty was signed which allowed Henry to keep his overseas gains and restored to him the French pensions, substantially augmented 'to recompense me [Henry] for witholdyng off myne inheritance' [163 *p. 41*]. A marriage between Henry's younger sister, Mary, and Louis was also arranged and took place in October. Thus, by the end of 1514, Henry had one sister as queen of France and the other as queen regent of Scotland; in addition he had forced Louis XII to acknowledge his claim to the French throne and his status as an international figure. On the debit side, however, his treasury was almost empty and his territorial gains were insignificant.

WOLSEY

Wolsey came to prominence and pre-eminence through the French war. His organizational skills had provided Henry with a well-equipped and relatively well-disciplined army in 1513. The king rewarded him with the bishoprics of Tournai and Lincoln in 1513. The next year Wolsey gave up Lincoln in return for the archbishopric of York, and in 1515 Henry appointed him Lord Chancellor. For the next fifteen years, Wolsey and Henry worked closely together discussing diplomacy and military plans. Although Wolsey has been depicted as the *alter rex*, in the field of foreign policy at least, he did not play an independent role. Certainly he gave advice to the king and his advice carried great weight, but no crucial decision was made by Wolsey alone. Henry, moreover, was often directly involved in the details of policy: almost all the diplomatic correspondence was either seen by him or made known to him in digest form; his hand appears on papers concerning war and diplomacy, while ambassadors' reports show that he was well-briefed in his long and serious audiences with them [25; 40]. How far then did Wolsey have a separate agenda from the king, and seek to pursue his own distinctive policies? What indeed were his motives and aims?

In his biography of Wolsey, A. F. Pollard argued that the cardinal aimed 'to hitch England to the Holy See' [77]. When Rome sought peace, Wolsey followed suit; when Rome made war so did England. Pollard decided that the reason for this subservience to Rome was Wolsey's personal ambition to become first cardinal, then legate and finally pope. This yearning for the papal tiara, he wrote, was 'the simple and straight thread' through the labyrinth of his foreign policy [77]. A close scrutiny of the evidence, however, does not substantiate this thesis. First, England's good relations with the Papacy were more apparent than real. At times, England's foreign policy demonstrated independence, even opposition to papal designs; as, for example, when Wolsey sabotaged the papal initiative for a crusade in 1518 and superseded Leo X's sponsorship of a five-year general truce in Europe by the Treaty of London which brought glory to Henry and himself. In addition, Wolsey neglected to build up and cultivate a party of supporters in Rome, a task which should have been the first priority of any hopeful aspirant to the papal tiara. He did not go out to Rome and he knew few curia cardinals personally. Nor did he try to secure favours or promotions for those lesser figures with whom he did work at the papal court. Furthermore, when the Papacy fell vacant in 1521 and 1523, Wolsey did not actively seek to fill the position but only reluctantly agreed to be a candidate when the king pressed him to put himself forward [117]. Finally, as already explained, Henry often paid close attention to the details of diplomacy, so Wolsey could neither control policy nor dupe the king into following a course of action which was not seen to be in the royal interest. Nor would Wolsey try to, for he could not afford to offend the king on whom he was totally dependent for his power.

Henry's best biographer, Professor J. J. Scarisbrick, has offered a more generous explanation of Wolsey's aims. The cardinal, he argued, sought peace throughout his political career. This was partly for the practical reason that 'war was the quickest way to lose money' but partly, too, because he was influenced by the New Learning and the humanist cries for an end to discord among princes. According to Scarisbrick, the 1518 Treaty of London, the tripartite conference at Calais and the meeting with Charles V at Bruges in 1521 were genuine attempts by Wolsey to bring about European peace. The fact that England went to war twice during Wolsey's period of political ascendancy, stated Scarisbrick, was not evidence against this interpretation of his policy but merely a sign that his policy failed [88] [*Doc. 7*].

There are, however, some important objections to this thesis. Too often Scarisbrick has taken Wolsey's own accounts of his actions at face value and accepted the sincerity of his general protestations extolling the virtues of peace. At the same time he has tended to ignore more specific comments made by Wolsey that were inappropriate for an apostle of peace: his 'triumphant description' in August 1523 of English brutal raids against the Scots, for example, or his expressions of approval when he heard in November 1521 that 'the affairs of the French king be like to decay' in Italy [25 *p. 44*; 40 *p.155*]. In addition, if one looks behind the words, Wolsey did not seem to be bringing peace to Christendom; rather, he was actively trying, before 1518, to check French power in Italy and after 1520 endeavouring to secure an Imperial alliance on the best possible terms. His determination at Bruges to delay declaring war on the French until the following year and his attempts at Calais to secure a truce with France were evidently devices to win time to prepare for war. Over the next year Wolsey was fully involved in military preparations, discussions of tactics to be followed and ways of resourcing the projected 'Great Enterprise' [25; 40].

A more general objection to Scarisbrick's interpretation is that it seems to misunderstand the relationship between king and minister; for there is no convincing evidence that before 1526 Henry was pulling in one direction and Wolsey in another. For this reason, historians are now arguing that Wolsey shared Henry's aims in foreign policy [25; 40; 157]. 'The important thing was to dominate affairs, and by this means bring honour and glory to his master – and of course to himself', explained Peter Gwyn [40 *p. 158*]. This quest for honour did not have to lead Wolsey and Henry into a policy of war. At times, honour might be better satisfied by an honourable peace and an international role as a peace-maker. Recognizing this, their policy was opportunistic and they veered between war and peace depending on the European situation, the reliability of their allies and their own ability to raise a large army [25; 40; 134; 135]. Once again in the words of Gwyn: 'All in all, the evidence is overwhelming that Henry and Wolsey set out to create an impression, not only at home but throughout Europe. Whether it was as warrior or peace-maker did not matter very much' [40 *p. 181*]. The following narrative is based on this interpretation of Wolsey's aims and strategies in foreign policy.

1515–29

The death of Louis XII on the last day of 1514 ended the brief entente between England and France. Mary Tudor, the royal widow, returned to England shortly afterwards as the wife of Charles Brandon, Duke of Suffolk, and the new French King, Francis I, aroused the jealousy of Henry by cutting a fine figure on the military field. At the battle of Marignano in September 1515 he defeated the renowned Swiss infantry and won Milan. Henry, unhappy at the emergence of such a dashing rival, was keen to build up a coalition against France. Wolsey speedily concluded an Anglo-Spanish treaty and dispatched Richard Pace as an envoy to hire Swiss troops who would fight alongside Maximilian and free Milan. For financial reasons Wolsey wanted to avoid open war at this juncture and preferred to find allies to put pressure on the French. Besides, Henry lacked any moral justification for attacking France [40; 157; 163].

The death of Ferdinand of Aragon in January 1516, however, led to a severe diplomatic setback for Henry and Wolsey. Ferdinand's successor, Archduke Charles of Burgundy, did not renew his grandfather's treaty with England but instead signed the Treaty of Noyon (1516) with the king of France. Soon afterwards, Maximilian too defected to the French camp and in 1517 concluded the Peace of Cambrai with Francis. Wolsey's diplomacy was in shreds. Not only had his plans for a new league against France ended, but also England was now diplomatically isolated. At the same time, Francis had demonstrated hostility to England by allowing the duke of Albany, heir presumptive to the Scottish throne, to leave France and stir-up trouble in Scotland. In these circumstances, Wolsey had little alternative but to repair relations with France. Anglo-French negotiations began in 1517 and an agreement was soon reached over maritime disputes and the problem of Scotland [88].

Meanwhile, Pope Leo X was anxious for a general European peace. Frightened by the westward advance of the Ottoman Turks, he argued that 'It is time that we woke from sleep lest we be put to the sword unawares' [46 *p.* 69]. In this frame of mind, he despatched legates to the Empire, France, Spain and England to arrange for a five-year truce among Christian princes and a crusade against the Turks. Cardinal Campeggio was named legate for England. The time was thus opportune for England and the Papacy to work together; and as Anglo-papal co-operation could bring prestige to Henry and rewards for Wolsey, both exploited the opportunity to the utmost. First, they sought to secure for Wolsey the legatine commission which Leo had refused to grant for four years. Campeggio was denied admission to England until Leo, realizing that his peace initiative would die if he did not give in, made Wolsey co-legate with Campeggio. Secondly, during Campeggio's stay, Wolsey continually upstaged and overshadowed the cardinal in small but significant ways to take over the role of chief legate [101]. Thirdly, Wolsey seized the diplomatic initiative and transformed the intended papal truce into an international treaty under his presidency. The Treaty of London which emerged in October 1518 was signed by all the major rulers and twenty lesser ones. They all pledged to keep the peace and to act together against any transgressor. It was a glittering success for Henry and Wolsey, whose fame as peacemakers spread throughout Europe [*Doc. 7*]. Two days later, Henry concluded a treaty with French commissioners which settled most of the difficulties between the two realms: Tournai was ceded to France in return for another yearly pension; Wolsey was compensated for his loss of the episcopal see 'by a large sum'; and Francis agreed to keep Albany out of Scotland. In addition, Henry's two-year-old daughter, Mary, was promised in marriage to the dauphin [33; 101].

As authors of the high-profile general peace, Henry's and Wolsey's honour and prestige depended on their success in acting as honest brokers in future international disputes to prevent the outbreak of war. Therefore they could not take sides when, on Maximilian's death, Francis I and Charles of Spain and Burgundy stood as candidates in the Imperial election. Yet Henry's pride dictated that he act to prevent Francis from winning the election. Consequently, in the mistaken belief that the pope would support him, Henry decided to present himself as a third candidate [88; 157]. Charles won the election and thereby became the most powerful ruler in Europe. His victory also made him suzerain of Milan and a consequent threat to French control of that duchy. In these circumstances, the peace proclaimed at London seemed unlikely to last. With war on the horizon, both Charles and Francis looked for a close understanding with Henry and each was keen to arrange a personal meeting with him. In the Treaty of London, plans had already been made for an audience between the English and French kings to seal their alliance of 1518, and a little later Wolsey had also extended an invitation to Charles to visit England. Now that both Francis and Charles were pressing for immediate talks, it was arranged that Henry should briefly see Charles in England, then sail to France for a longer meeting with Francis, and finally hold further discussions with Charles in Flanders in order to compensate for the brevity of the first meeting. In this way, Henry could display his even-handedness to both monarchs and continue to pose as the champion of peace [40; 157].

The meeting with Francis at the Field of Cloth of Gold (June 1520) was a splendid chivalric occasion much to Henry's taste, despite the fact that he was worsted by Francis in a royal wrestling match [89]. The discussions with Charles were more weighty and resulted in a treaty being signed in July 1520. This apparently committed Henry to very little, as he (and Charles) merely promised not to make any fresh alliances with Francis I for two years. Charles had hoped for more from England: at best, an agreement to mount a joint invasion of France, but neither Henry nor Wolsey thought the Imperial terms on offer were advantageous enough to risk the loss of face involved in abandoning the Treaty of London [40; 88].

The uneasy peace between Charles and Francis ended in 1521. During the previous autumn, Francis had taken advantage of a revolt within Spain to reconquer Spanish Navarre. At once Charles accused him of breaking the peace and appealed to Henry for help under the terms of the Treaty of London. Henry offered arbitration, which Charles initially accepted but Francis rejected. By the summer of 1521, however, Francis had suffered such military and diplomatic reverses that he was prepared after all to accept Henry VIII's offer of arbitration, and so a conference was arranged at Calais under Wolsey's chairmanship with no princes present. But Wolsey was now in no position to act as an impartial arbitrator since Henry had already decided to enter an Imperial alliance if the terms were right [40]. There followed an extraordinary sequence of events.

The conference at Calais opened in August 1521, yet two days after the arrival of the French representatives, Wolsey left Calais for Bruges where he negotiated a treaty with Charles. By the treaty, Henry promised to declare war on France if the fighting continued until November 1521 and to mount a joint campaign with Charles before May 1523 [88]. To cement their alliance, Henry's daughter, Mary, was to marry Charles instead of the dauphin. From Bruges, Wolsey returned to Calais to carry on his pretence at arbitration. He was anxious to avoid an immediate rupture with the French in order to give himself enough time to prepare for war. Furthermore, he wanted to keep his credibility as a peace-maker so that, when England entered the war, Henry would be able to claim that he was acting as defender of the Treaty of London [25; 40; 88].

Henry's and Wolsey's motives in joining the Imperial camp are difficult to fathom. Professor R. B. Wernham suggested that 'the explanation of Henry's undertaking to invade France with an army of 40,000 men is probably to be found in Charles's promise to marry Mary' [97 *p. 102*]. Henry, thought Wernham, was already worried about his failure to produce a son and wanted to marry his sole heiress to the strongest man in Europe. But Wernham's argument is unconvincing. As Henry knew, matrimonial agreements included in sixteenth-century treaties were often later overturned, and this dynastic arrangement was particularly fragile since Mary was too young to marry for several years. The attractions for Henry in forging an Imperial alliance lay elsewhere.

By 1521 it was clear that the peace negotiated in London would not last and that with it would disappear Henry's importance as an international peace-maker. Neutrality in the forthcoming war was not a policy which appealed to Henry, since it would reduce him to the role of onlooker in European affairs. Furthermore the London Treaty had stipulated that aid be offered to victims of aggression and it looked likely that Francis I would invoke this clause of the treaty if his war were to go badly against Charles V and his territories were invaded. There was, therefore, a risk that Henry would eventually be dragged into a war on the losing side or else lose face. An Imperial alliance would rescue him from this difficult situation and might also provide further opportunities for gaining new conquests and enhancing his prestige [40].

Some historians have argued that the Imperial-papal treaty of 28 May 1521 was an important influence on Henry and Wolsey in their quest for an alliance with Charles V. The pope, they have claimed, encouraged Henry and Wolsey to reach an understanding with Charles. Henry, therefore, viewed his alliance with the emperor as part of a wider league – a kind of crusade – against the pope's enemies, and saw himself as the saviour of Christendom. Wolsey, at the same time, hoped for more material rewards, in particular a permanent legateship [101; 157]. The evidence on this point, however, is far from clear, and Peter Gwyn for one thinks that 'the papal connection' was irrelevant in the formation of the Imperial league. As far as he is concerned, 'in responding to the Imperial proposals for an alliance Wolsey had no knowledge of the papal alliance with the emperor' and that during the Imperial negotiations 'Wolsey told the pope of what he was doing only after the moves had been decided' [40 *p. 156–7*]. The gaps in the sources are in fact too great for any certain conclusions here.

During 1522 and 1523 Wolsey made great efforts to obtain the necessary resources for war against France. War was actually declared on 29 May 1522 and in the same month the earl of Surrey led 15,000 men into Picardy. Unsupported by the Burgundians he could do no more than conduct a series of aimless raids. After this experience, Henry and Wolsey grew increasingly suspicious that Charles V would not meet his commitments as an ally. Without full Imperial support in the form of men and supplies from the Netherlands, the English could only mount a limited incursion, which might help the emperor by distracting the French from Italy but would not bring Henry the victory and rewards he desired. Some members of the Council, therefore, advised the king in July 1523 to abandon the 'Grand Enterprise' against France and turn instead to the conquest of Scotland, where the French were again using Albany to provoke anti-English policies. Henry himself oscillated between negotiations for peace and plans for an invasion [25].

In 1523, however, the mood changed with the treachery of Charles, Duke of Bourbon, one of the greatest noblemen in France. His rebellion against Francis I and offers of help to Henry opened up the possibility of large-scale military assistance, comparable to that given to Henry V by the duke of Burgundy around the time of Agincourt. Ever opportunistic, Henry and Wolsey acted swiftly. In July 1523 a new treaty was signed with Charles V, which agreed to an immediate joint invasion of France: an army of 15,000 from England; 5,000 from the Netherlands; and 20,000 sent by Charles V from Guienne. On 24 August 1523, 11,000 English troops under the duke of Suffolk landed at Calais and soon afterwards marched on Paris [133].

Suffolk's campaign was disastrous. Had Bourbon's army played its expected role, Paris would have been very vulnerable and Suffolk's invasion might well have succeeded. As it was, Bourbon failed to deliver a revolt in his own lands or an invasion of Champagne. His apparent defection freed the pressure on Paris and allowed French troops to withstand the English invasion. Henry's other allies also let him down: the troops from the Netherlands were unpaid and soon melted away; Charles V failed to open an offensive in Spain as he had promised. In addition, the severe weather greatly hampered the English troops on the march, resulting in desertions and even deaths from frostbite [133].

The English campaigns of 1522 and 1523 lost Henry the prestige he had hitherto enjoyed. The expeditions into northern France achieved little but cost more than Henry could afford, nearly £400,000. Not surprisingly, therefore, Henry and Wolsey began to lose confidence in the 'Great Enterprise' and to search for other strategies. The problem was that no attractive alternative was obvious. Henry could hardly desert his ally without losing honour and leaving England isolated in Europe. Making peace with France as a first stage in re-establishing the peace of Europe would also not be easy, as was manifest during secret talks with the French initiated in the spring of 1524 [40; 89]. Consequently, between late 1523 and early 1525, Henry and Wolsey seemed to be waiting upon events: they resisted pressure from Charles V for an English invasion of France, negotiated with the French, but remained pro-Imperial in the general direction of their policy [25].

The decisive battle of Pavia, when Charles V's army won Milan and captured Francis, propelled Henry and Wolsey into new plans for an invasion of France. When Henry heard news of Pavia on 9 March 1525 he was delighted; 'Now is the time for the Emperor and myself to devise means of getting full satisfaction from France', he declared [*Doc. 9*]. The following day the Council determined on war against France and a little later (21 March) instructions were issued for the levying of a non-refundable contribution to the royal war effort. This was called the Amicable Grant [115]. Henry's ambitions 'to subdue his auncient enemyes and to wyn and recover the realme of Fraunce' [115 *p. 196*] were foiled, however, by the negative attitude of both his ally and his subjects. Charles V refused to countenance Henry's proposal for a joint invasion which would end in the total dismemberment of France. At the same time, the Amicable Grant provoked such opposition that Henry was forced to abandon his grandiose scheme of invasion [25].

No wonder that Henry was ready by the summer of 1525 to withdraw from the Imperial alliance and make a separate peace with France. Not only had Charles proved an unsatisfactory ally during the campaigns of 1522 and 1523, he had denied England any fruits from the Imperial victory in Italy and then repudiated his marriage contract with Princess Mary. Moreover, Imperial hegemony in Europe was against Henry's interests. It would marginalize him in European affairs and exclude him from any future peace-treaty between France and the Empire. Consequently, Wolsey and Henry resumed negotiations with the French and concluded a small-scale 'diplomatic revolution'. On 30 August 1525, the two sides signed five treaties known collectively as the Treaty of the More, in which Henry agreed to give up his territorial claims to France in return for the annual pension. During early 1526 English diplomacy encouraged the formation of the anti-Imperial League of Cognac (made up of France and Italian states) and made provision for

Henry to become its 'protector', though not a member. In April 1527, by the Treaty of Westminster, perpetual peace was declared between France and England, a French marriage was arranged for Princess Mary, and Henry agreed to make war on Charles V if he refused to join the peace. The main purpose of all these alliances seems to have been to recover for Henry and Wolsey a central role in international diplomacy by imposing a peace settlement on Europe [40; 89].

By the summer of 1527, however, a new priority had entered English foreign policy. Alarmed about the succession to the English throne, Henry had decided to divorce his wife Catherine and marry Anne Boleyn. For this he needed the pope's assent but it was not easy to obtain, for Clement VII was not a free agent. The sack of Rome by Imperial troops in May 1527 had left him the prisoner of Charles V, Catherine's nephew, who strongly opposed the annulment. Even after his release in December, Clement still needed the emperor's goodwill to guarantee the independence of his territories. It seemed clear to Henry that the Imperial stranglehold on Italy had to be broken for the sake of his matrimonial plans, and he consequently entered a military alliance with the French king. In August 1527 Wolsey signed an agreement at Amiens which committed Henry to pay some of the costs of a French army advancing towards Italy. The following January, Henry reluctantly declared war against Charles and formulated plans to invade the Netherlands [40; 75; 101; 88; 135].

Neither Henry nor Francis were powerful enough to challenge the Imperialists effectively. When Charles's regent in the Netherlands responded to the invasion scare by suddenly ordering the arrest of all English merchants operating there, Henry and Wolsey caved in and made early moves towards negotiating a truce [135]. As for the French, their military successes of 1528 swiftly turned into a series of defeats in 1529. On 21 June, French troops suffered an irreversible defeat at Landriano, which forced the pope 'to become an Imperialist and to live and die as such' [5 p. 73]. A week later he and Charles V signed the Treaty of Barcelona and, as a direct consequence, Henry's divorce case was revoked to Rome on 12 July. The Treaty of Cambrai (August 1529) between Francis, the emperor and the pope ended French military efforts in Italy, left England isolated and cemented the Imperial-papal alliance. As a result, it was clear that Henry could not expect a favourable judgement when his divorce case was heard in Rome [75]. This failure of Wolsey's foreign policy did much to bring about his downfall in October 1529.

Wolsey was a showman on a grand scale but also a very skilful diplomat. In the words of one of his admirers, the papal nuncio in France: 'although in all his outward acts he shows excessive pomp and great ostentation, nevertheless in speaking, in behaviour and in negotiation, he reveals an intellect capable of every greatness, proper to any undertaking or affair because he is a dexterous and gracious man, full of glorious and noble intentions' [135 *p. 157*]. Contemporaries were impressed with his attention to detail in negotiations as well as the combination of temper-tantrums and conciliatory conversations which he brought to the negotiating table. When negotiating a treaty he knew when to compromise and when to stand firm, often marking on his papers the demands which he was prepared to give up and those which he held to be essential [135]. His ability brought him some success and for a short time he placed Henry at the forefront of the international scene. But the king had neither the military resources nor political influence to preserve that position as Europe drifted into war in the early 1520s. After 1522 Wolsey failed his master not because of any lack of skill but because England could only play at being a political giant. By 1525 England no longer had the resources to mount a continental invasion, and in the years following the battle of Pavia, Henry lacked the political clout to impose peace on a reluctant Charles V. Neither Wolsey nor Henry could see that France and Spain were two leviathans with whom England could not compete. Their vision was clouded by their personal ambitions and unrealistic dreams.

1529–40

From July 1529 until 1532 Henry worked hard to press the pope not to hear his divorce case at all. Royal agents in Rome were ordered to seek evidence from history that the pope had no jurisdictional rights over the king of England, and in June 1530 Henry sent Dr Edward Carne to Rome as an excusator to complain about the jurisdiction of the papal court [75; 88]. At the same time English envoys successfully urged Francis I to send an embassy to the pope on Henry's behalf. All to no avail. Clement, once so indecisive about the king's great matter, was now stiff in his resolve to hear the case at Rome.

In 1532 Henry thought it prudent to draw still closer to Francis I. It is not entirely clear whether he just wanted French cardinals to plead his cause at Rome or whether, as is more probable, he had already decided to break with Rome and thus needed French amity as a shield against papal and Imperial anger. In this pro-French policy he had the support of Anne Boleyn, who did much to encourage diplomatic and cultural exchanges between the two monarchs [150; 163].

Francis I responded positively to Henry's overtures; unwilling to accept as final the terms of Cambrai, which excluded him from Italy, he welcomed an alliance which could provide him with the means to close the Channel and cut off the Netherlands from Spain. But Francis also needed the pope's friendship if he was to win back influence in Italy, and so he was trying to arrange a marriage between his son, Henry, and the pope's niece, Catherine de Medici. The two kings, therefore, worked at cross-purposes. Francis was seeking to reconcile Henry and the pope by suggesting that Henry should marry Anne Boleyn in secret and then afterwards obtain the pope's tacit consent – a proposal which ignored Henry's need for an indubitably legal heir. Henry was hoping to persuade Francis to approve of, perhaps even follow him into, schism; a hope which depended upon weaning Francis from his aspirations to control Italy and which was thus completely out of touch with Francis's priorities [88; 163].

Nevertheless, for a time the two kings co-operated. In 1530 Francis pressured the Faculty of Theology at the Sorbonne into agreeing that the Aragonese marriage had been invalid. In June 1532 the two kings concluded a defensive alliance and in October they met at Boulogne and Calais. The French cardinals, Gramont and Tournon, were dispatched to work on Henry's behalf at Rome. But though these Franco-papal negotiations promised success, they went too slowly for Henry who, on discovering Anne's pregnancy in early January, married her publicly and proclaimed her queen. Francis was furious at Henry's untimely action, while Henry was equally outraged when Francis pressed ahead with his marriage alliance and entertained the pope for a month at Marseilles despite papal threats to excommunicate Henry. In fact the Franco-papal alliance was of advantage to Henry, for among other benefits it brought a delay in the sentence of excommunication [46]. Nonetheless Anglo-French relations deteriorated rapidly after the Valois-Medici marriage in October 1533 and 'disintegrated into bickerings about debts, religious differences, piracy and territorial infringements around Calais' [163 *p. 24*]. In 1535 Henry was even considering a renewal of the old alliances with the emperor [147].

Henry's breach with Rome and the attacks on papal supremacy in England, from 1533 to 1536, had revolutionary domestic repercussions. Their effects on the direction of foreign policy in the long term were far less fundamental but in the short term they severed the links between England and the Habsburgs and forced Henry to seek allies elsewhere. The greatest potential threat to Henry's marital and ecclesiastical policies clearly came from Charles V, who, it was feared, might use force to defend his religion, his aunt's rights, and his cousin Mary's claim to the throne. In fact, Charles was both unable and unwilling to intervene; the Turks and German Protestants kept him busy elsewhere, while his concern that the Netherlands' economy would be badly damaged by an interruption of trade with England led him to ask the pope in 1533 to refrain from placing an interdict on England, as that 'would disturb her intercourse with Spain and Flanders' [76 *p. 248*]. Nevertheless, Henry looked around for allies against Charles and, as his relations with Francis were still strained, his eye fell on the German Protestants, some of whom had formed the military Schmalkaldic League against the emperor. Contacts with them had been made as early as 1531, but negotiations did not become serious until 1533–34 when embassies were dispatched to Germany and Poland. Although the agents sent on these missions – Christopher Mont, Nicholas Heath, Robert Barnes and Stephen Vaughan – were all close associates of Cromwell, it was Henry himself who initiated this search for a Protestant alliance [36; 94]. His policy was not a success. The only alliance that emerged from the considerable diplomatic activity was an ill-conceived treaty with the revolutionary Protestant government of Lübeck in 1534. Hoping to gain some influence in the Baltic and facilities for recruiting German mercenaries, Henry agreed to send ships, men and money to help Lübeck place its own candidate on the disputed throne of Denmark, but the policy had to be abandoned after a year [36; 58; 94; 128]. Elsewhere, the negotiations with Protestants reached an impasse by 1530. The Lutheran princes, remembering Henry's title *Fidei Defensor*, did not trust his motives in entering a schism and demanded his subscription to the Protestant Confession of Augsburg as a preliminary to an alliance. Henry, for his part, was prepared to forget that the Lutherans had not supported his arguments for the divorce nor sanctioned his marriage to Anne, but was unwilling to make any doctrinal concessions [94].

By 1536, when the negotiations lapsed, the need for allies did not seem so acute. In that year, the renewal of fighting between Francis and Charles freed England from the dangers of isolation while the death of Catherine of Aragon both opened the way to an

Anglo-Imperial *rapprochement* and aroused hopes of a reconciliation with the pope. This sense of security was, however, short-lived. It was dispelled by the seemingly impossible event of 1538 – the conclusion of an amicable agreement between Francis and Charles. At Nice, in June, they signed a ten-year truce, and a few months later, at Aigues Mortes, they pledged themselves to co-operate against the enemies of Christendom. An immediate freezing of relations with England followed. In November, Charles raised difficulties about a projected marriage between his niece, Christina, and Henry. The next January, by the Pact of Toledo, Charles and Francis agreed to sever connections with England, and a month later they withdrew their ambassadors from London. At the same time, Pope Paul III published his bull deposing Henry (which had previously been suspended) and sent Cardinal Beaton to Scotland and Cardinal Pole to France in order to rouse support for a Catholic crusade [36; 142]. In reality, there was little danger of an invasion. Charles V had more pressing problems than that of Henry; Francis had no desire to act as a papal tool, while James V of Scotland was not prepared to make the first move. Perhaps most important, both Francis and Charles feared that the elimination of Henry would work to the other's advantage. But many in England believed the danger was real, though Henry himself seemed in less of a panic than his ministers, perhaps because he could not believe in the possibility of Charles and Francis working in concert for long. Nevertheless Henry reacted speedily on several fronts. The defences of the realm were put on an emergency footing at great cost to the Crown (paid for out of the 1539 dissolution of the monasteries). In order to avoid a Yorkist rising in defence of Roman Catholicism, Henry either imprisoned or executed the remnants of the Pole family in 1538 and 1539. The Act of Six Articles was passed in parliament to reassure conservatives who were unhappy with the previous drift of religious change. At the same time the hand of friendship was extended to any ruler at loggerheads with Charles V or the pope: the dukes of Urbino, Ferrara and Mantua, the king of Denmark, the duke of Bavaria and the princes of the Schmalkaldic League all received overtures from the king of England [68; 88; 94].

Henry's rather ludicrous attempts to find himself a fourth wife in 1538 and 1539, and his subsequent marriage to Anne, sister of Duke William of Cleves, one of the most powerful German princes, were also responses to the national crisis. William, although not Lutheran, had withdrawn his church from papal authority and so Cromwell opened the matrimonial discussions in January 1539 with the intention that it should be a positive step towards a Protestant alliance against the Catholic powers. Henry, on the other hand, saw the marriage in more limited terms as a device to end England's isolation [128; 161]. As soon as Henry saw his intended bride, however, he tried to back out of the venture. 'If I had known as much before as I know now, she should have never come into this realm', he told Cromwell in disgust after his first viewing [89 *p. 244*]. Had Charles V not been meeting Francis I in Paris the very day (1 January 1540) that Henry was meeting Anne, the marriage would probably not have taken place. At the same time, Cromwell was delivering warnings that Henry could not risk 'making a ruffle in the wind' for fear of driving Duke William into the arms of the two Catholic monarchs [89; 161]. But almost immediately after the wedding was concluded the marriage became otiose, for England's relations with Francis soon improved. In February 1540 Norfolk had been sent to Paris to entice Francis away from his unnatural entente with Charles and tempt him back into his earlier role as protector of Charles's enemies. The mission proved a success and the Cleves marriage, already personally embarrassing to Henry, became not only politically embarrassing for Cromwell but totally unnecessary for the security of the realm. It was even potentially dangerous as it might have drawn Henry into the maelstrom of German politics. No wonder Henry was so anxious to extricate himself from it, especially as his attention had already been caught by Catherine Howard [68; 88; 161].

The unfortunate Cleves marriage did not cause the fall of Cromwell in April 1540, as is sometimes suggested. Nevertheless it affected Cromwell's fortunes adversely. It made Henry lose confidence in his minister at a time when Cromwell's political position was being challenged by his rivals, Norfolk and Gardiner, and perhaps too it made Henry a prey to the charms of Catherine Howard, Norfolk's niece. Certainly Cromwell's reluctance to dissolve the Cleves marriage (because of Henry's choice for his fifth wife) shook the king's faith in his minister and made possible his fall [88; 161].

Even before Cromwell's execution, it was clear that the threat of foreign invasion had passed. Charles and Francis were already quarrelling and it came as no great surprise when Charles invested his son with the duchy of Milan and another stage in the Habsburg-Valois wars began. Henry was thus freed to reconsider his objectives.

7 MID-TUDOR ENGLAND 1540–63

INTRODUCTION

The traditional description of the reigns of Edward and Mary as a time of crisis has long been questioned. Initially, some historians extended the time-scale of the mid-Tudor crisis to include the last years of Henry and the early part of Elizabeth's reign as they realized that many of the signs of weakness evident under Edward and Mary were also present from at least 1540 until 1563. Now, however, the very designation 'mid-Tudor crisis' is being challenged and may very well soon fall into disuse [51]. No longer are the middle decades of the sixteenth century described as a period of chronic instability, mismanagement and political conflict. Co-operation and constructive responses to problems are the themes emphasized by historians today [51; 154]. Similarly, some of the political leaders of the age have been reassessed. Somerset, traditionally described as the 'Good Duke', so unusually tolerant in his religious beliefs and enlightened in his social policies, is now seen as a figure more typical of his age in demanding religious uniformity as the linchpin of order, and a practical social programme of reform for political rather than idealistic ends [26]. Northumberland, too, has been transformed from an overambitious, generally disastrous factional leader into a statesman of great stature [22; 113]. The focus of the new research has been mostly on the domestic political scene rather than on the making of foreign policy. Nevertheless, the reassessment of domestic politics has important implications for any discussion of England's relations with Europe.

In this section I have chosen to discuss together the mid-Tudor decades not because they represent a period of crisis when England's security was most vulnerable and government policies were unpopular and ill-considered. Rather, these years are discussed together because they mark the last time in the sixteenth century that the government embarked on Continental adventures in pursuit of dynastic interests. As such, they stand in stark contrast to the later reign of Elizabeth when, for all practical purposes, she gave up her intentions to acquire possessions in France by war (even though she did not renounce her claims formally). In addition these years saw a renewed interest and military involvement in the affairs of Scotland, providing a second element of continuity in foreign affairs across the mid-Tudor period.

1540–1547

In October 1542 Henry's troops invaded Scotland; four months later Henry made a secret alliance with the emperor which provided for a joint invasion of France within two years. In May 1544 the earl of Hertford mounted a major punitive raid into Scotland; the following month an English army of 40,000 men arrived in France. A strong link between events in France and Scotland is thus clearly indicated; but the nature of the connection is by no means clear and has been variously interpreted by different historians.

According to A. F. Pollard, Henry's main purpose in foreign policy after 1540 was the conquest of Scotland. This was, he argued, part of a coherent policy of unification and imperialism. Henry had already declared himself emperor in his own kingdom by denying papal supremacy, had integrated Wales into the political system of England and had been crowned king of Ireland. Thus, only Scotland needed to be absorbed into England for Henry's vision of a united British Isles to be realized. The war against France, continued Pollard, was secondary to this greater purpose and was only made necessary by France's traditional friendship for Scotland and consequent aid to the Scots [76]. Pollard's conclusion was based upon scholarly research, but it is no longer satisfactory in the light of modern interpretations of Henry's reign. In the first place, Henry is now seen as a traditionalist not an innovator; and in an age when political frontiers were the result of inheritance rather than geography it is unlikely that he was far-sighted enough to envisage the British Isles as a political entity. He certainly did not demonstrate the same prescience in his view of Calais; although geographically part of France, he never considered it as anything other than English. Moreover, the shiring of Wales and conversion of Ireland into a kingdom were responses to specific political situations and not the working out of a grand design [88].

Perhaps because he is appreciative of these objections to Pollard's interpretation, Professor Wernham has restated Pollard's idea in a different form. He re-emphasized the point that Henry's policy was directed primarily against Scotland but saw Henry's aims as fundamentally defensive. Scotland, linked by ties of friendship and marriage to France, was a great threat to England's security. Henry's fear was that James V would use his claim to the English throne (he was the son of Henry's elder sister) to throw England into confusion were Henry to die leaving under-age heirs. Wernham suggests that it was this security threat, not imperial dreams, that led Henry to seek mastery within the British Isles. Had Francis not planned to provide assistance to the Scots, he concluded, Henry would not have embarked on the war in France [97]. Professor Scarisbrick was not, however, convinced by Wernham's analysis. 'It is very arguable that concern for Scotland during the last years of his reign was secondary to his preoccupation with France and that, as in 1513, he looked to the North only because he was about to plunge into the continent' [88 *p. 425*]. In other words Scarisbrick believed that the reopening of the Habsburg-Valois wars in 1542 gave Henry his opportunity to return to the quest for military glory and territorial gain in France. The campaign against Scotland was but an attempt to fasten his backdoor before leaving for France.

Scarisbrick's scenario is very attractive. It is easy to imagine Henry, his manhood undermined by the revelations of the infidelities of his wife, Catherine Howard, seeking to regain his zest, dignity and glory by returning to his youthful dreams of conquest in France. Quite possibly too he was spurred on in his ambitions by younger courtiers who were restless for military adventure – and France provided much greater and more conventional opportunities for glory than Scotland. Nevertheless, as Dr M. Bush has pointed out, 'Henry VIII's war against Scotland did not simply derive from his war against France'. Though the two wars were connected 'connection did not mean encapsulation' [26 *p. 9*]. Just as it is a mistake to see the war against France as an offshoot of the Scottish war so it is wrong to assume that there would have been no war in Scotland had Henry not planned to fight against France. Henry had other motives for launching an attack on Scotland in 1542. During the dangerous years of the 1530s, James V had demonstrated that, despite Henry's careful wooing of him, his loyalties were to France and Rome rather than to his English uncle. He had twice married French princesses, the second of whom, Mary of Guise, was being courted by Henry himself. He harboured the political rebels who fled to Scotland after the failure of the Pilgrimage of Grace. He ignored Henry's patronizing advice to seize ecclesiastical lands and break with the pope; instead Cardinal Beaton, a papal agent, remained the most influential figure at James's court. Perhaps most important of all, James gravely insulted the English king when in September 1541 he failed to keep an appointment to meet Henry, then on his northern progress at York. Henry, who had been left waiting in vain for nine days, was predictably furious and no doubt determined to teach his young nephew a lesson [137]. Henry's decision to renew the Continental wars, however, clinched the matter. James V's conduct demonstrated that it would not be safe to leave Anglo-Scottish affairs unsettled before leaving for France.

As a result, Henry sent ambassadors and an army of 3,000 to the North in August 1542. These ambassadors presented humiliating demands to the Scots while the army stood in the wings, ready to act if the terms were not accepted. Although the Scots were in a conciliatory mood, their hesitation in accepting all the terms gave Henry the pretext to send his troops over the border. The raid was intended to intimidate and overawe James V but at first it had the opposite effect. James appealed to Rome for support and organized a force against England. The result was disastrous for Scotland. At Solway Moss, the Scots suffered an ignoble defeat; there were few casualties but many leading men were captured. Three weeks later James V died leaving the Scottish throne to his one-week-old daughter, Mary [88; 137]. Had Henry so wanted, he could have easily invaded, conquered and incorporated Scotland into his kingdom. Why did he not do so? Wernham has argued that fear of the French deterred him from immediate action and that the amassing of ships, troops and supplies (intended for Scotland) at Rouen made Henry decide to take direct action against France rather than invade his northern neighbour [97]. But in fact the number of French troops intended for Scotland was small; Paget, then ambassador to Paris, informed Henry, in January 1543, that 2,000 men were destined to sail from Normandy [37]. They were only a token gesture because the last thing Francis wanted was war with England just when he was preparing for action against Charles. This Henry surely realized, and if he had wanted to conquer Scotland the way was open for him. By this time, however, he was looking forward to resuming his military exploits in France and was negotiating an alliance with Charles V for this purpose. Consequently, he preferred to subdue Scotland by other means – by a more circuitous route. He planned to use those Scottish lords captured at Solway Moss as the nucleus of a pro-English party in the Scottish government. They were liberated on the express understanding that they would bring the Scottish queen to England, arrange a dynastic union of the two realms through her marriage to Henry's heir, Edward, and act as Henry's agents in Scotland. Even after the earl of Arran, heir presumptive to the Scottish throne, became governor in January 1543, Henry believed that he could control Scotland by means of his agents, for Arran seemed to be sympathetic to Henry's policies [88; 137].

But Henry had misjudged the situation. His knowledge of Scottish affairs was slight and he did not heed the advice of those who were better informed [*Doc. 10a*]. Sir Ralph Sadler, Henry's envoy in Edinburgh, warned him of the intensity of Scottish sentiment against an imposed union, explained the complexity of the Scottish political scene and pointed out the need to move cautiously. Yet Henry pressed hard for the young Queen Mary to be brought up in England, which merely aroused Scottish suspicions. He also had a misplaced confidence in the loyalty and power of Arran and the pro-English faction, and preferred threats to promises as a means of getting his own way. Consequently, the Treaties of Greenwich concluded in July 1543 formally betrothed the two children but did not bring Henry the immediate benefits of securing the custody of Mary and committing the Scots to the renunciation of all their alliances with France. As the summer progressed, opposition to the pro-English party grew in Scotland so that by August the country seemed on the brink of civil war, and in September Arran deserted the English cause. The final blow to Henry's policy came in December 1543, when the Scottish parliament repudiated the Treaties of Greenwich and renewed all previous treaties with France. In retaliation the king ordered his commander-in-chief Edward Seymour, Earl of Hertford, to carry out a punitive raid into Scotland. Henry refused to occupy some strategic towns which would have helped him keep out the French and re-enter Scotland whenever he might choose, as Hertford advised. Instead he ordered Hertford to sack Edinburgh, Leith and St Andrews so that 'the upper stone be the nether and not one stick stand by another' [88 *p. 443*]. This Hertford had achieved by May [1] [*Doc. 10b*].

Henry's decision to send only a small army into Scotland temporarily was the result of his concentration on the French war which by then was his main priority. Events in Scotland had prevented him launching a full-scale offensive into France in the summer of 1543. Only a small force of 5,000 men under Sir John Wallop had entered the Boulonnais to help in the defence of the Low Countries. A major campaign was, however, planned for the summer of 1544. Thanks to the success of Hertford's raid it was set in motion in June, when over 40,000 men left for Calais. Henry's commitment to the venture is apparent from the manpower devoted to the enterprise. His enthusiasm can likewise be seen in his determination to be present with his army despite pressure from his councillors and the Imperial ambassador for him to stay safely at home. The campaign was shambolic even by the generous standards of the time, for Henry did not define his objectives until a full week after the vanguard of his army had arrived at Calais. Even before setting off Henry had already begun to question the wisdom of the Anglo-Imperial strategy to march on Paris, but he had not yet decided what to do instead. Caution deterred him from advancing too far from his supply base in Calais, while the quest for honour and territorial gain, as well as distrust of his allies, led him to prefer to seize towns alongside the Calais Pale [134]. At last, on 20 June, he ordered Norfolk to lead part of the army to besiege Montreuil; and a little later, Suffolk was sent to lay siege to Boulogne. Norfolk's army failed but Suffolk entered Boulogne on 18 September. Meanwhile, the Imperial troops, despite some setbacks, marched on through Champagne unchecked by a French force (except at the siege of Saint-Dizier and a skirmish near Soissons). Francis held his main army in reserve for the defence of Paris and tried to divide his enemies by extending unofficial peace-feelers to each. Henry for his part would listen to no peace proposals until he had captured Boulogne; but Charles, short of money and disappointed by Henry's independent actions, responded positively and signed the Treaty of Crépy with Francis on the same day as Boulogne surrendered to the English [88].

Henry was thus left to continue the fight alone against Francis. 'From then on, the war between the two kings became personal in a way that no previous campaign had been' [162 *p. 295*]. Peace talks began in the autumn, and to Henry's chagrin Charles V acted as a mediator, but the negotiations broke down because of Henry's refusal to return Boulogne and his insistence that the French abandon the Scots. As an agreement seemed out of the question, Francis vowed 'to win as much as the Englishmen had on this side of the sea', and planned a two-pronged attack: to capture a town on the south coast of England for which Boulogne might be exchanged, and to send his troops to Scotland to facilitate an assault on England from the north [162 *p. 295*]. Henry's position looked exceedingly vulnerable. He had no allies, for his desperate approaches to the German princes had evoked little response and it looked as if the Catholic world would be united at a papal General

Council due to assemble in December 1544. Furthermore, Henry's funds were running out and he had to fall back on further expropriation of church wealth and loans from Antwerp. Scarisbrick wrote that, 'England now faced a threat greater than that of 1539, greater than any, perhaps, she had known for generations, or would know again until Philip II threatened her' [88 *p. 454*].

In fact the danger was a chimera. Francis, like Henry, could not afford a long, large-scale war and he had no intention of mounting an invasion of England. Charles V was planning to fight the German Protestants and would not become involved in the minor Anglo-French conflict. Henry, moreover, had prepared well against any invasion force: the outlying ring of castles, recently constructed along the south coast, were impressive defensive structures, and Henry's navy contained both well-armed carracks and fast, oared vessels [55; 143; 144].

On 31 May 1545 a French expeditionary force landed in Scotland where it was welcomed by the Scots, who were sickened by the destructive raids carried out regularly from England. On 16 July a large French fleet left Le Havre and a few days later sailed into the Solent. In the skirmishes that followed, the *Mary Rose* sank with the loss of 500 men, not as the result of French guns but after water had poured through her open gun-ports. On 21 July the French landed on the Isle of Wight but only burned several villages before they were forced to withdraw. Another brief exchange of fire occurred near Beachy Head, after which the French retired to Le Havre. The French attempt to besiege Boulogne failed. Action on the Scottish front was equally uneventful; the Scots, after drawing close to the border, withdrew without doing any damage and Hertford carried out yet another punitive raid in the Lowlands [97; 143; 162]. In the words of one contemporary French commentator, Francis 'had been at great charge and nothing done' [143 *p. 29*]. Alexander McKee has attributed the French king's failure in the south to an overambitious plan and the ill-discipline of his forces, as well as to Henry's own skill as a military commander. The English king personally directed the naval campaign from Portsmouth, and, throughout, retained a firm control over his navy and army. He was also remarkably successful in anticipating and blocking each of the French commander's moves [143].

By September both sides were keen to resume peace. In June 1546 the Treaty of Ardres was signed whereby England was to retain Boulogne until 1554, when it was to be restored complete with the new fortifications built by the English in return for 2 million écus to be paid by the French. In addition, France was to pay England all the pensions owed under former treaties. It was a compromise which was only acceptable to the two sides as a short-term measure because they could not afford to continue the fight. Consequently, the treaty did not bring an immediate improvement of relations between the two countries. Lord Lisle, following oral instructions from his king, destroyed French fortifications near Boulogne after the treaty was signed. In November, Francis sent some help to Scotland when it looked as if Henry was about to mount another raid. Nevertheless, when Henry died in January 1547, an uneasy peace existed with both France and Scotland [88; 162].

Henry's last wars cost far more than those at the beginning of his reign, due partly to monetary inflation but more to their growing scale. According to the most reliable figures which have been compiled, the total cost of the war against France and Scotland was £2 million. The war could not be financed by taxation alone; hence the heavy sale of Crown lands and feudal rights after 1540, the debasement of the coinage (1541–46) and the borrowing of large sums on the Antwerp money market from 1544 [38]. But not only Crown finance suffered. The wars resulted in a contraction of trade and contributed to the decay of old-established industries by starving them of capital investment. The increase in the pace of inflation in the mid-Tudor years also owed much to the war; both the debasement of the currency and increase in government expenditure worked to raise prices. Although the metal industries, especially the manufacture of cannon, were stimulated by the war and provided opportunities for employment, overall the wars had an adverse effect on the Crown's finances and the English economy. In short, in so far as there was an economic crisis in the 1540s, the war played a significant part in creating it [45; 51; 102].

EDWARD VI 1547–53

Henry VIII's death brought about a change of emphasis rather than a change of direction in foreign policy. Lord Protector Somerset (the erstwhile Earl of Hertford), like Henry, aimed at the dynastic union of Scotland and England through the marriage of Edward to Mary Stuart. Both men's purpose was to satisfy their honour and safeguard the kingdom; neither thought in idealistic terms of national consolidation. Somerset, like Henry, resorted to military action when the marriage policy failed, not in order to assert direct control of Scotland but to punish disobedience. Again like Henry,

Somerset tried to win over a group of Scottish noblemen who might give 'assurances of their support for the union'. Nonetheless, the Scottish war of Somerset differed in two vital respects from the wars of Henry. First, whereas Henry considered the Scottish problem as secondary to his concern with France, for Somerset the war against Scotland was the main priority. He thus sought peace with France to give himself a free hand in Scotland. Secondly, while Henry relied on a series of large-scale raids into Scotland to secure obedience, Somerset – who was only too aware of their military ineffectiveness since he had been responsible for executing them in Henry's reign – sought instead, to place permanent military garrisons there as a means of enforcing his policy [26].

Initially Somerset tried to win his way in Scotland by negotiation. In late 1547 and early 1548 he made diplomatic overtures to individual Scottish lords but these were in the main unsuccessful. At the same time, he tried to encourage Protestantism in Scotland, a policy which also failed, possibly because he went about it in an unsustained, half-hearted way. Indeed, how sincere Somerset was in these early attempts at a diplomatic, conciliatory solution is a matter of some debate [26; 47]. It seems most likely that he went through the motions of non-military methods without having much faith in their successful outcome. He was certainly planning to use force at this time. Plans were afoot to establish military forts in Scotland. France was wooed in an attempt to keep her neutral. In March 1547 Francis I signed a treaty with Somerset, and on his death, discussions were opened with Henry II, his successor, about the sale of Boulogne before the stipulated date (1554). But Henry II, more bellicose than his father, repudiated Francis's treaty and demanded not only the return of Boulogne but Calais too. Therefore the talks collapsed, for Somerset would not yield part of the king's patrimony [161]. At the same time Somerset was trying to keep Charles V's friendship, since his goodwill was needed for the supply of foreign mercenaries from Flanders. Furthermore, should France aid the Scots, Somerset wanted to ensure that French ships would be unable to use the Netherlands' ports. With these ends in view, Somerset tried to present himself to the Imperial ambassador as a religious conservative and delayed the introduction of religious reform. Here his policy was more successful; Charles V was inclined to be friendly, and Anglo-Imperial amity deterred Henry II from declaring war on England immediately and sending a very large army to Scotland [26].

Nevertheless, Henry II was determined to prevent the pro-French party in Scotland from succumbing to English pressure. Accordingly, in June 1547 he dispatched Leo Strozzi there with a few thousand men and some artillery. These French reinforcements seized some military strongholds and it looked as if France would soon dominate Scotland. As a result, Somerset invaded with 18,000 men in September 1547. Although the Scots rallied, they suffered an overwhelming defeat at the battle of Pinkie. Now Somerset felt ready to implement fully his garrisoning policy; English garrisons were established on the islands of Inchholm and Inchkeith in the Firth of Forth, at Broughty Castle in the mouth of the Tay, and at Hume and Roxburgh Castles in the East Marches. By April 1548, Dundee, Arbroath, Dumfries and Haddington had been added to the list of garrison towns. The garrisons were intended as centres from which reprisal raids could be launched. By this means Somerset planned to protect England's friends among the Scottish nobility and put pressure on the Scottish government to agree to the marriage of their queen, Mary, and Edward VI.

At the same time Somerset continued to try to win the friendship of the Scots. Tracts, such as the *Epistle to the Nobility of Scotland* – which Professor Jordan has used as evidence of Somerset's idealistic and moderate approach – were in fact pieces of propaganda produced at this time to justify the English government's policy. Bibles were distributed and preaching was encouraged to attract the Scots to the Protestant and English cause. Ultimately, however, force became the order of the day because the Scots would not submit and proved perfectly capable of harassing the garrisons, even before the French arrived to give them aid [26].

After the battle of Pinkie, Henry II became increasingly concerned with the affairs of Scotland. He could not afford to see the disappearance of an ally and thus took up the status of 'Protector of Scotland'. In June 1548, 10,000 French troops landed in Scotland, occupied Edinburgh and carried off Mary Stuart to marry the dauphin in France. Her arrival was greeted enthusiastically by Henry II who ostentatiously treated her as a daughter and boasted that France and Scotland were now one country [97; 161]. Somerset did not adapt his Scottish policy to meet this major challenge from France. He simply hoped that Henry II would soon tire of the expense and pull out. Consequently, he continued to rely on the policy of garrisoning instead of employing a naval blockade and invading once again with a large royal army. But, although the garrisons were able to hold their own against the French, they were not large enough to defeat them or to provide sufficient protection for the Scots who had given 'assurances' to the English. By late

1548 the 'assured' Scots were changing allegiance and helping the French. To make matters worse, the garrisons were proving so expensive that an annual invasion would have cost less. Somerset spent over £580,000 in two years, which was almost double the cost of Henry VIII's five years of war in Scotland [103]. Somerset had valued garrisons for their relative cheapness as well as their effectiveness, yet on both counts he was proved wrong.

Although French hostilities soon spilled over into the Boulonnais, Henry II did not declare war until August 1549. The summer risings in England, and Charles V's refusal in July to give assurances that he would help England to withstand any future French attack on Boulogne, dispelled Henry's earlier caution. The campaign itself was heavily influenced by the fact that Henry had delayed fighting until the summer, whereas the beginning of the campaigning season was usually in the spring. The French were unable to invest the forts around Boulogne until late August and the onset of heavy rains in early September put an end to the campaign without the recapture of the town.

The fall of Somerset in October 1549 made the earl of Warwick (soon to be duke of Northumberland) the dominant figure in the Council. Warwick's main aim was to restore order in the country and for this he needed peace abroad. Somerset himself had realized that the war had to be brought to an end, and it seems that he was about to open negotiations with the French when his protectorate collapsed. Warwick, as early as November, decided to sell Boulogne and in this policy he had the support of Paget and other members of the Council [37]. The issues for negotiation were how much the French would be prepared to pay for the town and whether Henry II would agree to continue paying the pension to the English king. The final treaty which emerged in January 1550 was described by Jordan as 'the most ignominious treaty signed by England during the century', the result of a policy of 'peace at any possible price' [48 *p. 116*]. Many contemporaries too considered the treaty a blow to national pride; the contemporary allegory *Philargyrie* scorned Warwick for having 'sold for ready gold forts that were builded strong'. Yet, Dr Potter's thesis and article on the diplomacy of the peace have concluded that the treaty was not a French *diktat*; rather, that Henry II was forced to step down from the extreme demands he had initially made. For example, Henry had originally stipulated that he would only pay 159,000 écus for Boulogne yet 400,000 écus were finally agreed as his payment. Furthermore, the treaty allowed the English to remove the equipment and munitions provided by them since 1544. The terms of the treaty therefore, argued Potter, while undoubtedly confirming the military advantages built up by the French in the two preceding years, were not the unmitigated disaster and humiliation for the English which might have been expected at the nadir of English fortunes during the summer of 1549 [146; 161]. In matters of prestige, too, England's face was saved when a convenient formula was found to shelve the pension dispute. In fact the French pension was never again paid but the English did not concede their right to it. The treaty, moreover, was the only realistic outcome of a ruinous war which was causing financial collapse and internal instability. As Paget, one of the peace negotiators, explained in February 1550, the war was causing 'the evil condition of our estate at home ... Then yf the disease wil not be taken away, also warre (whiche is one cheife cause) must be taken away' [141 *p.125*].

Northumberland's agreement with France at Angers in 1551 was a similarly realistic response to England's problems. Knowing that England could no longer afford to fight her ancient enemy, Northumberland was prepared to patch up a friendship in the hope that it would deter Henry II from attacking Calais. He did not sell England's interests for the price of maintaining his own personal ascendancy at home, as Jordan suggested [48]. Rather, he and his Council decided their first task must be to repair the damage wrought to the country's finances by the Scottish and French wars. Peace with France was the outcome; it may not have been glorious but it was expedient and with hindsight appears as an act of statesmanship [22].

MARY 1553–58

Mary's foreign policy has been customarily viewed as the most disastrous element in a disastrous reign. Her marriage to Philip II of Spain and the consequent Habsburg alliance provoked such bitter discord in England that they resulted in parliamentary protests, factional strife, one major rebellion and numerous conspiracies. England during her reign became the new battleground of Habsburg and Valois kings, as the French and Spanish ambassadors competed for influence at the Marian court, while the French, after the Habsburg marriage, conspired with her enemies [42; 52]. The alliance with Spain drew England into the final stage of the Italian Wars with the calamitous result of the loss of Calais. Even now, when Mary's reign is being presented in a more positive light, the traditional picture of her foreign policy has been little modified. In the essay on foreign policy in a volume reassessing mid-Tudor polity, C. S. L. Davies concluded that: 'Lack of enthusiasm for the war, lack of inspiration on Philip's part, bad leadership by the Council, bad morale, or worse, among the defenders of Calais, go a long way towards explaining the sorry results of the French War' [124 *p. 185*].

Mary's decision to marry Philip lay at the heart of her foreign policy. Yet the marriage was not as ill-conceived as hindsight suggests. Dynastic and religious considerations meant that Mary had to marry to produce a Catholic heir, but there were few eligible candidates for her hand, and only two were considered seriously: Edward Courtenay, Earl of Devon and of Yorkist descent, and the Archduke Philip, eldest son of Charles V. Though the preferred choice of the anti-Habsburgs, Courtenay was a man of little worth; Simon Renard's condemnation of him as 'proud, poor, obstinate, inexperienced, and vindictive' is generally thought a fair judgement by historians [103 *p. 89*]. There is certainly nothing to indicate that the earl would have been a better choice for Mary. Philip, on the other hand, had much to recommend him as a husband. As Paget argued, England could use the Habsburg alliance as protection against Henry II of France who coveted Calais and had built up a strong Scottish alliance. Political stability might also be more easy to maintain with the promise of Imperial troops to suppress disorder whenever necessary. Commercial ties with the Netherlands made the marriage economic good sense [37]. According to her biographers, however, Mary's own determination to marry Philip rested less on these political and economic considerations than on an emotional attachment to his father, Charles V. From the moment of her accession, Mary demonstrated the warmth of her feelings towards the emperor, who had protected her during the reigns of her father and brother. In private audiences with Simon Renard, the Imperial ambassador, she thanked Charles for his past help and promised him 'to follow your advice and choose whomsoever you might recommend' as a husband in the future [5 xi *p. 132*]. Yet, in truth Mary required some persuasion before she agreed to accept Charles's proposal that she marry his son, an offer he made in order both to further Habsburg interests against France and, perhaps more importantly, to help Philip in asserting his claim to rule the Netherlands after Charles's death. The prestige of an English title and a power base in northern Europe would strengthen Philip's hand against the rival claims of Charles's brother and nephew.

The Habsburg marriage was thus a policy which can be defended as politically desirable as well as personally pleasing to the queen. But Mary's method of negotiating the marriage was perhaps unwise. Although there was little indication of fervent anti-Spanish feeling at the outset of her reign, Mary initially preferred to conduct the negotiations with the Imperial ambassador privately, even clandestinely, rather than openly in full Council. For three months the Council heard rumours of the match but they were not properly informed of Mary's intentions until 27 October 1553. During this period of uncertainty two political groupings arose at court: one led by Paget in favour of the marriage; the other by Gardiner who opposed it and wanted the queen to marry Courtenay. How severe the conflict was between the two groups is a matter of some debate [42; 52; 152; 154]. Recent research argues that, at worst, there were only 'clamorous differences of opinion' [154 *p. 60*]. Even if this is true (and the evidence is not clear-cut) the weight of Council opinion against the match probably did much to influence the thinking of lesser figures at court – men such as Croftes, Throgmorton, Carew and Wyatt who became prepared to rebel as a means to thwart the marriage. Furthermore, the manner in which Mary had closeted herself with the Imperial ambassador lent substance to the fears that Mary would in future listen to Spanish advisers instead of to deserving Englishmen. The strong opposition to the marriage came as something of a surprise to some observers and is indeed difficult to explain. Renard, the Imperial ambassador, told Philip that antipathy to Spain had been provoked by the intrigues of the French, the heretics and the nobility who favoured Courtenay [*Doc. 12*]. Paget believed that the antipathy stemmed from 'the fears entertained by the English that his Highness, if the Queen were to die without heirs, might try to make himself King of England' [5 xi *p. 393*]. There was also the natural concern in a patriarchal society that Mary would defer all decisions to her husband and that consequently Englishmen would be excluded from patronage, and that England would be drawn into the war against France.

The marriage treaty allayed some of these fears. While Mary lived, Philip's powers were strictly curtailed within the realm: he was to enjoy all Mary's titles but policy-making and the exercise of patronage were reserved for the queen. Furthermore, it was explicitly stated that 'The Realm of England by occasion of this matrimony, shall not directly or indirectly be tangled with the war that is' [124 *p. 160*]. If Mary were to die without issue, Philip's titles and rights would die with her, but if Mary produced a son he would inherit England, the Netherlands and Franche-Comté. Spain would also be his, if Philip's son by an earlier marriage died without heirs. Were Mary to die leaving a young heir, Philip was to have little influence over the upbringing of his child. These terms were so favourable to England that they were announced to Mary's subjects by royal proclamation on 14 January 1554 in order to win over public opinion [152]. Thus, far from being paralysed into inactivity by dissensions about the marriage, the opposition within the Council to the Habsburgs was apparently channelled constructively into devising safeguards to protect the realm against a foreign king [154]. Mary herself, it has been argued, played her part in this diplomatic success; by harping on the domestic opposition to the match, she was able to persuade the Imperialists to make concessions which at the outset had seemed unobtainable [152].

The worst of the opposition to the marriage was over by February 1554. Neither French interference nor English protests could prevent Philip's safe arrival in July 1554 and the marriage ceremony on the 25th. It is true that anti-Habsburg sentiment did not subside after the wedding and expressed itself in propaganda (for example, *A Warnyng for England*), minor tumults and parliamentary opposition to Philip's coronation [6]. There also remained misgivings about Philip's influence over policy. His attempts to stop the Guinea trade caused resentment and there were fears that he would draw Mary into his European wars. Yet the opposition to the marriage should not be exaggerated; after the failure of Wyatt's rebellion, no further rebellion shook the reign and, although English malcontents, such as Henry Dudley and the Killigrew brothers, clustered around the French court and plotted the deposition of Mary, their plots were foiled with ease [52]. Indeed, there was no strong reason for any resurgence of concern about a foreign king. During Philip's brief visits to England, all the court ritual asserted Mary's role as sovereign and emphasized that her husband was merely her consort.

The marriage did not at first have a great impact on foreign policy, for Mary, like her councillors and subjects, had no wish to go to war. Consequently, to avoid the obligation to fight for her husband's cause, she sent Paget and Gardiner to La Marque near Calais in May 1555 to arrange a general peace. Although this attempt at mediation failed, France and Spain patched up their differences at Vaucelles in February 1556, when they signed a five-year truce without involving England in the negotiations. The Truce of Vaucelles was treated by the English Council as a calculated snub but in fact it brought Mary some benefit. Henry II of France's enthusiasm for the plots of Dudley and his fellow conspirators noticeably waned as the danger of war with England subsided; and this partly explains their failure [52].

But the truce lasted only a short while. Conflict between Pope Paul IV and the Imperialists in Italy led to military action there in September 1556, and the duke of Guise soon afterwards set out for Italy with a French army to help his ally, the pope. When in January 1557 the French breached the truce in Flanders, Philip called for English aid. On such an important issue Mary could not act alone without consulting her Council. The majority of councillors came out unequivocally against intervention: it was against the terms of the marriage treaty, they argued; the country could not afford a war; and the threat of sedition made it 'very daungerous to entangle them now with new warres especially where necessitie of defence shall not require the same' [53 *p. 242*]. Philip, however, was determined to obtain England's full support and arrived in England in March to achieve that end. Paget had already declared himself in favour of the war, but only three or four councillors supported him and Philip had great difficulty in winning the others over. It was only the raid on Scarborough Castle at the end of April by Thomas Stafford and the exiles from France that induced the Council to change its mind. Indeed so fortunate were the timing and results of Stafford's raid that Professor Loades has wondered if 'Stafford's apparently harebrained and provocative venture was not connived at or even prompted by Paget and his agents' [53 *p. 367*]. Henry II certainly publicly disclaimed any responsibility for such a mis-conceived adventure: 'I bade him [i.e. Stafford] beware as I already saw him without his head if he persisted in these ideas of his' [79 *p. 353*]. Nonetheless, the French king had in the past sponsored or encouraged a number of plots against the queen, and allowed pirates to operate from his ports and prey on English shipping in the Channel. Philip and Paget, therefore, had no difficulty in persuading the Council that they could not ignore the provocation of the raid. War was officially declared on 7 June [37; 51].

'Seldom, if ever, has England gone to war so unwilling and so unprepared,' wrote Professor Wernham [97 *p. 231*]. In fact, once war was declared, the queen's subjects rallied around the government. Noblemen and gentlemen who had been implicated in rebellion or sedition willingly took commands in the army and navy in order to return to favour. Sir Peter Carew, Sir James Croftes, Sir Nicholas Throgmorton, William Winter and the three sons of the duke of Northumberland were but a few of the ex-conspirators who fought for Mary in 1557 [124; 130]. The difficulties experienced in raising troops were the result of both the inefficient muster system and the famine of 1555–57 rather than a reflection of popular hostility to the war. Although there were men who refused to pay the 1557 forced loan, £109,000 was collected by it – an amount not much lower than the sums brought in by each of Henry VIII's forced loans in the 1540s. The parliamentary subsidy of 1558 raised £168,000 which was as much as the government had wanted, and the objections voiced in that parliament were not to voting supply in itself but to committing the country in advance to taxation for 1559 [124; 132].

The fighting at first went well. On the Continent a small English force under Pembroke took part in the successful siege of St Quentin in August 1557, and although it arrived after the worst of the fighting, its performance attracted favourable comment. On the Scottish borders, Shrewsbury was able to contain minor incursions and the Scots failed to respond to Henry II's call for an invasion of England [*Doc. 13*]. By October 1557 the campaign seemed to be over; the pope had accepted the Spanish terms and Philip's army was preparing for winter. But the dry weather continued and Henry II decided to try to recoup his prestige after the humiliation of St Quentin by an enterprise against Calais. He recalled the duke of Guise from Italy, and in January 1558 Guise's army attacked and captured Calais within eight days [*Doc. 14*]. Many explanations have been postulated for the speedy fall of the fortress. Responsibility immediately fell on the deputy of Calais, Lord Wentworth. He was charged with (and in 1559 acquitted of) treason. Although he can justly be accused of undue complacency in the face of danger, he did not betray the garrison to the French. Mary's economy drive has also been held to blame for the disaster; the castle of Calais was in need of repair although the outer defences were satisfactory. More importantly, the garrison was run down after August to save money. It was thus only at peacetime strength when assaulted, and contained barely half the number required for minimum security against attack. To counteract Guise's invasion, therefore, reinforcements were needed, but these were not forthcoming as the Council, unable to believe that Calais was seriously threatened, failed to send a relief army to Wentworth before 1 January. Philip, too, did not order his army to aid Calais; he only sent 200 arquebusiers on 6 January [124].

Calais, once lost, could have been recaptured. Indeed, Philip urged a military effort to recover the Pale and offered to use his own

Netherlands' army in the campaign. By this time, however, the Council was too demoralized to respond positively. The financial cost, the difficulty of raising troops, fear of attack from Scotland were all arguments put forward to reject Philip's plan. The Council's co-operativeness was possibly not helped by the fact that the Spaniards' payment of English pensions was 10,000 ducats in arrears. Furthermore, the Council had other grievances against Philip II. He had refused to sever relations with the Scots at the time when a Scottish invasion seemed imminent. Nor would he assist the Merchant Adventurers in their periodic quarrels with the Hanseatic League; on the contrary he wanted to uphold the League's claims to privileges which were unacceptable to the English Council. Other seemingly trivial disputes also served to convince the councillors that Philip had no concern for English interests and that they in turn should not sink their resources into another campaign on behalf of Spain [5; 53; 124].

The war, nonetheless, continued. Though the recapture of Calais was not attempted, a large-scale attack was mounted against Brest in the summer, but this failed dismally. Peace negotiations began in May 1558 and by October it was becoming clear that a settlement would be reached which left Calais in French hands. Before a treaty was drawn up, Mary died and the peace conference was adjourned until her successor was crowned. Philip followed the terms of the marriage settlement, withdrew gracefully from his English title and allowed Elizabeth to inherit the throne. The fears of the original opponents of the marriage, therefore, were unrealized.

ELIZABETH I 1558–63

Elizabeth inherited a realm which seemed especially vulnerable to attack. Although peace negotiations had begun at Cateau-Cambrésis, France and England were still technically at war, while French troops were in Scotland and the French Dauphiness, Mary Stuart, declared herself to be the legitimate Catholic claimant to the English throne. The pope had already declared Elizabeth a bastard, thereby giving the French a mandate to invade [6]. Elizabeth was consequently dependent on England's alliance with Spain as a means of protection. The Spanish alliance was, however, by no means sure. Philip might make a separate peace with France and, if the pope went on to excommunicate Elizabeth, might even join in a crusade against her. Nevertheless, Elizabeth thought that she could rely on Philip's support. Her diplomats assured her that it was against

Spanish interests for the French-backed Mary Stuart to replace her as queen of England – and they were right. 'If England were lost, it cannot convincingly be denied, though some would dispute it, that these lands of Flanders themselves would be in imminent danger,' argued a policy directive written for Philip in 1559 [46 *p. 50*]. Consequently, despite Elizabeth's early demonstrations of committed Protestantism, there was a strong basis for Anglo-Spanish co-operation, and Philip promised to safeguard English interests in the peace negotiations reopening in February 1559 at Câteau-Cambrésis.

The main stumbling block to peace was the future of Calais, since initially Elizabeth would not agree to accept its humiliating loss. But it soon became clear to her that Henry II would not surrender the town without a fight and Philip would not employ troops for its recovery. Hence she decided to negotiate a compromise directly with Henry and in March accepted a face-saving formula: the French would hold Calais for eight years and then would either return it to England or pay a sum in compensation. The French also made other concessions, agreeing to include Scotland in the treaty and pull down the fortress of Eyemouth on the Scottish borders.

The Treaty of Câteau-Cambrésis was signed on 2 April 1559. According to the late Sir John Neale, its conclusion freed Elizabeth from the necessity of appearing conservative in religion in order to keep the Spanish alliance and allowed her subsequently to permit a full reformation of the English church. A review of the evidence by Norman Jones, however, has shown that the signing of the treaty had no influence on the making of her religious settlement. Nor did the Elizabethan church settlement have any immediate impact on relations with Spain, for Philip continued to protect Elizabeth at the papal court and to seek a Habsburg marriage alliance with her [69; 46; 35].

Furthermore, the conclusion of peace hardly improved relations with France. The loss of Calais and the marriage of Mary Queen of Scots to the dauphin created a strategic nightmare for the English government; in the words of Dr Dawson: 'An English bridgehead in France had been replaced by a French bridgehead in Britain' [125 *p. 201*]. Few English statesmen, moreover, doubted France's hostile intentions towards Elizabeth. Henry II continued to uphold his daughter-in-law's claim to the English throne and strengthened French influence in Scotland. Consequently, many of Elizabeth's councillors were delighted at the news that Scottish Protestant nobles had rebelled against the pro-French and Catholic policies of the Regent, Mary of Guise, in 1559. Their delight was tempered by the fear that French reinforcements might be dispatched to help the regent crush the Scottish rebels.

To counter this threat, the queen's Secretary, William Cecil, wanted English help to be sent to the rebels. His short-term objective was to remove French influence from Scotland and secure England from invasion. In the longer term, however, he hoped to establish a Protestant Anglophile government in Edinburgh which would then forge a close political alliance with England. It is possible that his plans also included the deposition of Mary and the union of the two neighbouring realms [125]. But these objectives were kept secret from Elizabeth whose outlook was quite different. Although the queen allowed warm messages of support and £2,000 to be sent to the Protestant lords, she refused to countenance the deposing of Mary or the dispatch of an army to Scotland. Paramount in her mind was the maxim: 'It is against God's law to aid any subjects against their natural prince' [97].

Developments in France, however, forced her hand. The death of Henry II in July 1559 brought Mary Queen of Scots to the French throne as the wife of Francis II. Her uncles, the duke of Guise and the cardinal of Lorraine, dominated the new king and were determined to stamp out the rebellion in Scotland and assert Mary's claim to England. In August and September they sent 2,000 French soldiers to Scotland while Elboeuf (another Guise) stood by ready to send a further 8,000 or 10,000 men as necessary. The Scots, powerless against the French, appealed to Elizabeth for aid [92].

In December 1559 the Council met to discuss the question. Cecil, naturally, supported military action to assist the Protestant lords, and Pembroke, Clinton, Howard and some others agreed with him. Nicholas Bacon, however, led a group who feared the dangers of war against France and preferred to give secret, indirect aid until the spring to see what happened; while the duke of Norfolk argued that Elizabeth should marry an archduke of Austria and enjoy the security of a Habsburg alliance against France instead of dabbling in Scottish politics. Elizabeth was reluctant to commit herself openly to the rebels whose Protestantism and politics were too radical for her tastes. Initially she agreed only to order Admiral Winter to sea with instructions to intercept Elboeuf's reinforcements. The news that French troops had reached Leith soon persuaded the more conservative councillors that more direct intervention was necessary, and on 24 December the Council advised the queen to send an army northwards to help the Scots to expel the French. Elizabeth, however, refused to endorse the dispatch of troops, and she only gave way when Cecil threatened to resign if the Council's advice was not taken. Only then did she agree to send the duke of Norfolk to Newcastle to command her northern army [59; 85; 103].

Landed operations were still ruled out until the outcome of Winter's mission could be assessed. The Admiral's fleet reached the Firth of Forth in January 1560 and cut off the lines of communication between the French garrison at Leith and the main French forces in Fifeshire. It was decided, however, that more than a naval blockade would be required to flush out the French. Elizabeth therefore agreed at the Treaty of Berwick in February 1560 to give the Scottish lords protection, but 'only for the preservation of the same in their old freedoms and liberties from conquest during the time that the marriage shall continue betwixt the Queen of Scots and the French King and one year after' [97 *p. 255*]. At the end of March, Cecil authorized Lord Grey to lead English troops into Scotland. Grey joined with the Scots in an advance against the French stronghold at Leith, but his campaign went badly and a grand assault on the garrison in early May ended in a humiliating failure. With the death of the Scottish regent on 11 June 1560, however, the French agreed to negotiate. On 6 July, English and French commissioners signed the Treaty of Edinburgh which provided for the withdrawal of both English and French forces from Scotland and the renunciation of Mary's right to use the English arms and title [97]. It remained unratified by Mary Stuart. Nonetheless, in practice it broke the Auld Alliance and left the Protestant lords in control of the government of Scotland [125].

Cecil's adventurous policy had paid dividends and the subsequent establishment of Protestantism in Scotland closed that country to French influence until the end of the decade. Elizabeth's caution had also contributed to the successful outcome. She had effectively, if unknowingly, delayed military intervention until a propitious time, when Guise power in France was being challenged by the Huguenots. The result was that the Guises were prepared to make terms with Elizabeth in order to concentrate on their problems at home.

The political struggles faced by the Guises in France gave England security for the next year. The death of Francis II in December 1560 and the seizure of the regency by Catherine de Medici brought moderates to power who had no wish for a conflict with England. In March 1562, however, civil war broke out in France and by July it looked as though the Guises would triumph. In desperation Huguenot leaders pleaded for Elizabeth's aid, and offered in return immediate possession of Dieppe and Le Havre as pledges for the eventual cession of Calais. Elizabeth demonstrated no signs of the hesitation and reluctance to act which she had displayed in 1559. She had been unhappy at accepting the loss of Calais at Câteau-Cambrésis and had unsuccessfully tried to reopen negotiations for its future at the Edinburgh talks in 1560 (her instructions arrived after the treaty had been signed). The possible recovery of Calais attracted her to the Huguenot cause at least as much as the fear of a Guise victory [*Doc. 15b*]. For her councillors the issues were different; Cecil was most concerned with the security angle [*Doc. 15a*]; Robert Dudley, the queen's influential favourite, supported an interventionist policy to forward his own political ambitions; while others (including England's ambassador in France, Sir Nicholas Throgmorton) were motivated by religion. But, although their priorities might have differed, the queen and Council were agreed on a policy of military intervention in France. By the Treaty of Hampton Court (September 1562) Elizabeth promised loans and troops to the Huguenots [59].

The war went badly for England. First Rouen and then Dieppe fell to the Catholics before the end of the year. The final humiliation came when the Huguenot leader, the prince of Condé, who had been captured by his enemies in December, patched up his disagreements with Catherine de Medici and agreed to help her expel the English from France. At the beginning of June 1563, French troops moved towards Le Havre, the last English garrison. In mid-June the town was beset by plague and in desperation the earl of Warwick, its commander, surrendered on 29 June 1563. Thereafter Elizabeth abandoned any hope of retaking Calais by force of arms, and viewed with suspicion proposals for continental adventure. Her caution was shared by Cecil.

8 ELIZABETH 1564–1603

For the first decade of Elizabeth's reign, England's relations with Spain were uneasy but not especially strained. Neither Philip nor Elizabeth wanted to sever the traditional Anglo-Habsburg friendship. Philip II, for all his Catholicism, preferred a heretic to a French woman as queen of England and so twice during the 1560s dissuaded the pope from excommunicating Elizabeth. Similarly, at the council of Trent his cousin, Emperor Ferdinand, refused to countenance Pius IV's proposal to recognize the title of Mary Queen of Scots to the throne of England. Elizabeth, for her part, wanted peace with Spain to counteract the danger of hostility from the Guises in France. Consequently, despite mutual suspicions and the trade embargo of 1564, there was no open breach between England and Spain before 1568. On the contrary, efforts were made to negotiate a matrimonial alliance between Elizabeth and the Archduke Charles of Austria for the purpose of strengthening Anglo-Habsburg accord. During this time cordial relations were greatly assisted by the presence of Guzman de Silva as Spanish ambassador at Elizabeth's court, a man who was greatly liked by the queen and adept at smoothing over minor irritations [35; 147].

The breach of 1568 was not the result of a new hard-line Catholic attitude in Spain towards England. Despite appearances to the contrary, the expulsion of John Man, the English ambassador, from the Spanish court in April and the replacement in September of De Silva by Guerau de Spes, a friend of English Catholic exiles, should not be taken as signs of a new direction in Spanish foreign policy. Dr Man, a married Protestant cleric, who was reported to have called the pope 'a canting little monk', was hardly a wise choice of diplomat for Spain and it was perhaps surprising that Philip tolerated him for three years. Similarly, the transfer of De Silva to Venice was not at all sinister; it had been requested by the ambassador himself, since four years was a long time to spend in such an arduous and expensive posting as ambassador to England [98]. His replacement, moreover, was instructed by Philip 'to serve and gratify' the queen, and to try 'to keep her on good terms' [5 *pp. 67–8*]. With the Netherlands in political turmoil, Philip could not afford to lose the friendship of the queen of England.

The origins of the breakdown in Anglo-Spanish relations lay in the events occurring in the Netherlands between 1566 and 1568. Whereas under Charles V the Netherlands had been a loose dynastic confederation of semi-autonomous provinces and cities, under Philip II more centralized rule was imposed. When a revolt broke out in 1566, Philip responded by sending the duke of Alva with an army of 10,000 men, later augmented to 50,000, to suppress it. Elizabeth's attitude to this turn of events was ambivalent. On the one hand, her dislike of rebels led her to approve publicly the executions of the principals, Egmont and Horn. On the other, she perceived grave security dangers in the presence of Spanish troops in the Netherlands; for the deep harbours and the prevailing winds made that country an excellent springboard for an invasion of England, and once Alva completed his task of restoring order and extirpating heresy he might well be tempted to try such a venture [98].

By the end of 1568 a crisis was approaching; Alva had achieved a military victory over all his opponents including Louis of Nassau and William of Orange. There were few options open to Elizabeth to combat this danger to England's security. War was out of the question for England did not have the military power to face Alva on equal terms, and the dangers of sending a small force to aid the Netherlanders were apparent to anyone remembering the 1562–3 fiasco in France. Harassment of Spain and a demonstration of England's power may have seemed the only viable policy. One method of doing this was to encourage the attempts of seamen to break through the Spanish trading monopoly, and perhaps the last of John Hawkins's slaving voyages should be seen in this light [*Doc. 2*]. During the 1560s Hawkins made three voyages to West Africa, where he purchased or seized slaves, and then sold them in Spanish America. In so doing, he was breaking the trading monopoly of the Portuguese king in West Africa and that of the Spanish king in Spanish America; yet some of his ventures were financially backed by high-ranking court officials, including Lord Admiral Clinton and Robert Dudley, while Elizabeth herself invested in the second voyage and tacitly approved the third. Greed was no doubt a powerful motive but the 1567 slaving venture was a substantially more powerful expedition than its predecessors and 'it may be that the queen wished to impress the king of Spain by a veiled threat of her own power and his vulnerability' [19 *p. 125*]. If so, it was an ineffectual gesture. The voyage ended in disaster when Hawkins's ships were destroyed by the Spaniards in the harbour of San Juan de Ulúa in September 1568 [19].

Another opportunity to harass the Spaniards arose in 1568. In November Spanish ships containing about 400,000 florins in cash took refuge from bad weather and Channel privateers in English ports. The money was a loan from Genoese bankers to be used to meet some of the cost of Alva's army in the Netherlands. Elizabeth at first seemed ready to provide a naval escort to protect the ships on their journey. Then, after Cecil had learned that the money legally still belonged to the Genoese bankers and was not yet Philip's, he issued orders for the bullion to be brought ashore. Recently, Professor Ramsey has argued against the long-held view that Cecil's action was a preliminary move in a plan to seize the treasure; on the contrary, claimed Ramsey: 'The treasure was to be landed as an act of Anglo-Spanish collaboration to preserve it from the French' [82 *p. 93*]. The evidence is certainly by no means clear-cut, but it is hard to believe that Cecil's intentions in issuing the orders were entirely benign. It is far more likely that once he had learned of the money's legal status and heard the news of 'the massacre' of San Juan, which had reached London early in December, he was considering the possibility of the queen taking over all, or some, of the Genoese loan herself. If so, his motive was to make life as difficult as possible for Alva in the Netherlands. What was at stake for him was not just the money but the security of England and the future of the whole Protestant cause in Europe [59; 85]. Neither he nor Elizabeth had strong reasons to expect violent reprisals from Philip; seizures of ships on one pretext or another were common in the sixteenth century and an English appropriation of the bullion was not indefensible in law.

De Spes soon suspected that Elizabeth and Cecil intended to retain the treasure for their own use. In a panic, without waiting to discover the truth, he prematurely urged Alva to seize English ships and property in the Netherlands [*Doc. 16*]. This Alva did with some misgivings, and immediately the English government retaliated in kind. Philip II also seized English ships and goods in Spanish ports. The result was a total suspension of Anglo-Spanish trade which was to last for almost five years [82]. A diplomatic blunder was, therefore, principally responsible for the first major breach between England and Spain.

As a result of the bullion affair, relations deteriorated between the two governments. For a time, Philip gave support to Elizabeth's enemies: he authorized Alva to encourage and give money to the Catholics of the North in 1569, though he drew back from committing himself to their cause when he realized their weakness. In 1571 he was enthusiastic about the Ridolfi plot and instructed the more cautious Alva to send 10,000 soldiers to England in support of the Catholics. At the same time, he listened to Thomas Stukeley's plans for an invasion of Ireland. Elizabeth, too, was more openly hostile to Spain. English privateers co-operated with the Netherlands' Sea Beggars* and Huguenots in attacking and looting Spanish ships. In 1571 negotiations were opened for a marriage alliance with Henry Duke of Anjou, heir presumptive to the French throne, and, when this failed, a defensive treaty of friendship was signed with the French at Blois in 1572 [35]. Nevertheless, Elizabeth did not want the breach with Spain to last, no more did Alva. Just before the Treaty of Blois was signed, the queen indicated her readiness to begin negotiations to reach an agreement over the restoration of commerce. At the same time, in another conciliatory move, she took action to curb the privateering of the Calvinist Sea Beggars, who were operating from English ports, and they were forced to leave these safe havens in early 1572 [35; 153].

At last, in March 1573, a limited agreement for two years was reached whereby Anglo-Spanish trade was reopened. The next year, England and Spain signed the Convention of Bristol [82]. This improvement in diplomatic relations caused the queen to withdraw her support from maritime ventures in the Spanish Indies, and she would not grant a licence to Richard Grenville to embark on a new voyage of discovery in 1574. The English raids which continued in the Indies were entirely private in character until 1577 and did not appear to be a major cause of friction between the Spanish and English governments [19].

The prospects of a continuing accord between England and Spain were to be shattered by events in the Netherlands. In April 1572, the Sea Beggars unexpectedly captured the town of Brill in Zealand which resulted in the reopening of the revolt of the Netherlands [153]. Spanish attempts to subdue the Protestant rebels there aroused the fears and religious zeal of Englishmen; at the same time Elizabeth's escalating policy of interference provoked the anger of the Spaniards. This was to be the main reason for the war which broke out in 1585.

Elizabeth's handling of the Netherlands crisis is a matter of some controversy. Professor Wernham has argued that Elizabeth followed a consistent policy towards the Netherlands for the rest of her reign. It was, he writes, a policy built on fear of France as much as on fear of Spain. 'She wanted to retain Spain as a counterpoise to France. She wanted the Netherlands, though restored to their ancient liberties to remain Spanish so that they would not become French' [97 *p. 320*]. In recognizing England's limited military resources, she intended to avoid open confrontation with Spain and hoped to secure her objectives by offering mediation between the two sides or by providing indirect aid to the rebels if they seemed in danger of total defeat. Although ultimately she was forced to go to war, in Wernham's view she was both far-sighted and successful in her policy. On the other hand, Professor Wilson has described Elizabeth's policy as 'a bewildering succession of expedients' [104 *p. 16*]. He has drawn attention to her vacillating and inconsistent policies: at times offering financial support then withdrawing it; first objecting to French intervention then sponsoring the Anjou expedition. Furthermore, he doubted the queen's sincerity in calling for the restoration of the Netherlands' liberties; and although he accepted as genuine her fear of France, he considered it exaggerated and groundless. Finally, he judged her policy to be a dismal failure. Her prevarications, he argued, drove the rebels into the arms of France in 1581, while her refusal to support Orange in 1577 hastened the divisions in the rebel ranks, for only her military support could have given him sufficient military stature to quell noble opposition to his power [104].

In his detailed study of Elizabeth's policy Professor MacCaffrey has presented both a more complex and more convincing view than either that of Wilson or Wernham. Unlike Wilson, he detected consistent principles in her foreign policy towards the Netherlands. On the negative side, she did not seek dynastic expansion and regularly turned down opportunities to acquire Continental lands as the price of her support for the rebels. Positively, she was concerned with national defence: first, to prevent France expanding into the Netherlands and thereby controlling the coast from Brittany to Groningen; second, to persuade the Spanish government to accept a religious and political compromise which would include the removal of Spanish troops and a return to provincial autonomy. Yet, unlike Wernham, MacCaffrey saw Elizabeth at the mercy of events rather than the initiator of a consistent foreign policy, for while her principles remained constant, she was compelled to react in an *ad hoc* fashion to changes in the international situation over which she had little or no control. Elizabeth's policy, he wrote, was 'largely reactive in nature, responding to the ebb and flow of events across the North Sea'. She was always ready to bend to the realities of events and to live 'from day to day . . . improvising as the situation demanded' [60 *p. 193*].

An analysis of Elizabeth's responses to events in the Netherlands demonstrates the validity of MacCaffrey's thesis. The three years following the rebel seizure of Brill seemed to offer little hope of an eventual Spanish defeat. Only two provinces, Holland and Zealand, were in revolt, while the Spanish army was experienced and well-commanded. Accordingly, despite both popular support in England for the rebels, as seen in the public celebrations of their capture of Middelburg in 1574, and pressure from the prince of Orange and his influential supporters at Elizabeth's court (Leicester and Walsingham in particular), the queen was determined to maintain a policy of 'ostentatious neutrality' and to offer herself as an impartial mediator. At times she did give hidden help to the rebels by allowing them to recruit English volunteers and to purchase supplies, while also preventing English mercenaries from entering Alva's service. Nevertheless, she consistently refused to give Orange official aid; there was little advantage in alienating Spain irrevocably on behalf of a small band of rebels who seemed destined ultimately to come to terms with their king [60].

Only during the second half of 1575 did Elizabeth's policy begin to change direction. In that summer the Spanish successfully launched a new military offensive. It looked as though either the Spanish army would soon triumph or that the rebels would call in the French in a desperate bid to save themselves. Anxious to forestall both possibilities, Elizabeth made new overtures to the Spanish government. She offered again to mediate; but this time, significantly, she laid down the terms she required as part of a reconciliation settlement: the restoration of the Netherlands' ancient liberties and the removal of foreign troops. On religion she was equivocal; probably she envisaged Catholicism as the official religion with the Protestants being granted freedom of worship in private. Had these terms been accepted, the Netherlands would have returned to the political situation under Charles V, and this would have posed no security threat to England. By specifying conditions that she considered necessary for England's security, Elizabeth was stepping away from the position of neutrality carefully established since 1572. Nonetheless, she still resolutely refused to give open aid to the rebels and, when Holland and Zealand offered her their sovereignty in November 1575, she turned them down [13; 60].

The events in the Netherlands during 1576 drove Elizabeth along the route of active involvement in the revolt. The Spanish army's mutinies of that year, which culminated in the sack of Antwerp, terrorized the local population and pushed all seventeen provinces into open rebellion. An Estates-General* representing the whole Netherlands was summoned and in October drew up an agreement with Holland and Zealand, known as the Pacification of Ghent. As the opposition to Spain was no longer confined to two provinces but extended to the whole of the Netherlands, the Estates appeared a more acceptable ally to Elizabeth. Furthermore, the Pacification called for the expulsion of foreign troops and the restoration of the provinces' ancient liberties – the very terms sought by Elizabeth. As a result, Elizabeth promised the Estates a loan of £100,000 if the Spanish government refused to accept the Pacification. In fact, due to lack of money, the new Governor-General of the Netherlands, Don John, had little choice but to accept. In February 1577 he signed the so-called Perpetual Edict. In April the Spanish army left the Netherlands for Italy.

Elizabeth's diplomatic victory was short-lived. War broke out between Don John and the Estates in the summer of 1577 and the Spanish troops were recalled. There were also rumours that a French army would be sent to aid Don John, while Elizabeth's spy network discovered that Don John was plotting with Mary Stuart. The danger to England's security seemed to require drastic remedies. Accordingly, Elizabeth promised the Estates an immediate £100,000 and offered them English troops if and when the French forces arrived. At the same time she warned Philip that if he did not accept the Pacification and recall Don John, she would give military aid to the rebels. In this policy Elizabeth had the full support of her Council [72; 73].

Philip neither accepted the Pacification nor recalled Don John; yet Elizabeth did not send an English army to the Netherlands. Why not? First, the response of the Estates to her offer had been less than satisfactory. They had shown reluctance to accept English soldiers and, without informing Elizabeth, had invited Archduke Matthias to act as their governor-general. Secondly, the factionalism developing among the Estates, and the military weakness they displayed at the battle of Gembloux in January 1578 against the army of Don John, made them appear unreliable allies. Thirdly, Elizabeth's Council, so recently united, began to offer conflicting advice. Leicester and Walsingham continued to press for intervention, but Sussex, for one, pointed to the danger of entering into a war against Spain. Elizabeth listened to the voices of caution and drew back from open intervention [60; 158] [*Doc. 19 (a) and (b)*].

Nevertheless, Elizabeth could not afford to leave the Estates to their fate, for it might mean their total submission to the military power of Spain or their rescue by ambitious leaders in France. As Sussex wrote, 'the case wylbe harde bothe with the Queen and with Ingland yf ether the Frenche possesse or the Spanyardes tyranyse in the Low Contryes' [*158 p. 353*]. After another unsuccessful attempt to mediate, she decided in April 1578 to hire John Casimir of the Palatinate to fight for the Estates with 11,000 mercenaries. Before Casimir's arrival in the Netherlands, however, Francis, Duke of Anjou, the French king's brother, entered Hainault to aid the rebels. In August the Estates granted him the title 'Defender of the Liberties of the Low Countries' [35; 44]. Casimir arrived soon afterwards; but instead of leading a united Estates-General against the Spaniards, he became involved in aiding the radical Calvinists against the Catholic Malcontents,* thus intensifying the religious tensions among the Netherlands' rebels [73].

By the summer of 1578 Elizabeth's foreign policy in response to the Netherlands crisis was in disarray. The Spanish government had consistently rejected her offers of mediation and was deeply suspicious of her intentions. The rebels, enfeebled by religious, political and personal differences, looked unable to hold their own against the Spaniards. Anjou was embarking on a military adventure in the Netherlands which might result in French territorial gains. Elizabeth had managed to alienate the Spaniards without aiding the Dutch or keeping out the French. It is difficult to understand how Professor Wernham could include this period of her foreign policy in a chapter entitled 'High water mark' [97]. The marriage negotiations which Elizabeth opened with Anjou in the summer and autumn of 1578 were a desperate attempt to improve the situation. At best Elizabeth hoped that, if the marriage took place, pressure by France and England on Philip would lead to a settlement in the Netherlands along the lines of the Pacification of Ghent. At the very least she saw the marriage as a means by which she could control Anjou. Initially, she planned to use the offer of an English crown as bait to entice him from military adventures and satisfy his appetite for glory. After his visit to England in August 1579, however, she realized that she could not divert him from the Flanders project but hoped instead to use his troops as agents of English policy. In the event, the marriage negotiations came to nothing; but the personal contact which Elizabeth had established with Anjou during their course alleviated her fears about his character and ambitions to such an extent that she was prepared to send him financial assistance in September 1580 and to sponsor his 1581 expedition to the Netherlands [35; 60].

But it was not only her confidence in Anjou which brought about this new direction in foreign policy. The dramatic growth of Spanish power between 1579 and 1581 had convinced Elizabeth that Anglo-French co-operation was required 'to impeach the King of Spain's greatness' [10 *p. 353*; 35]. In 1580, Philip II invaded Portugal and the following year was recognized as king by the Portuguese Cortes.* At a stroke he had acquired another rich colonial empire and also a substantial fleet which gave him the resources to mount a seaborne invasion of England. His designs on England seemed confirmed by Spanish support for two Papal expeditions to Ireland in 1579 and 1580. On the Netherlands front, the policy of Alexander Farnese, Prince of Parma, the new Spanish Governor-General, was transforming the military and political situation to the advantage of Spain. By 1581, he had reached agreements with the South Walloon provinces (southern Flanders, Artois and Hainault) and the Catholic Stadtholder* of the north-eastern provinces, and was ready to begin his reconquest of the north.

Elizabeth, consequently, pursued more openly anti-Spanish policies, while at the same time trying to avoid open confrontation with Spain. Not only did she subsidize Anjou, but she proposed an Anglo-French league designed to support small-scale enterprises in Flanders and Portugal against Spain. Henry III, she believed, though staunchly Catholic, had a similar interest in containing the ambitions of the Habsburgs. She also welcomed Dom António, the pretender to the Portuguese throne, at court and contemplated sending a force to the Azores on his behalf. In 1580, amid public celebration, she knighted Francis Drake for his maritime exploits against the Spaniards. Anti-Spanish sentiment was so strong that the Spanish ambassador was either ignored or treated with contempt at court [35; 60; 98]. Elizabeth's policy was largely unsuccessful. Henry III of France would not assume an anti-Spanish stance, while Anjou in the Netherlands proved a disaster. Philip II tightened his grip on Portugal by completing the occupation of the Azores in 1583, and Parma won victory after victory in Flanders and Brabant. The deaths of Anjou and William of Orange in June and July 1584 seemed to remove the last obstacles to the restoration of Spanish power in the Netherlands and the consequent invasion of England [73].

The death of Anjou had other important repercussions. It left the Protestant Henry of Navarre as heir presumptive to the throne of France and so opened the final phase in the French religious struggles. To prevent Navarre's eventual succession, the Catholic League and the Guises concluded in secret the Treaty of Joinville (December 1584) with Philip II in which he promised the Guises his protection and subsidies. The danger to Elizabeth was acute. In the first place, with the Guises in his pocket, Philip looked upon the claims of Mary Stuart with more favour. Secondly, there was no longer the power of France to check the overmighty Spain.

Even before the Treaty of Joinville was made known to Elizabeth, she had hoped to persuade Henry III to take up the role of protector of the Dutch. In February 1585, however, Henry had turned down the offer and thrown the responsibility for aiding the rebels back on England. In the following month Elizabeth heard rumours of the treaty, which exposed the threat to England's security [60; 98]. These circumstances led Elizabeth to offer informal aid to the Dutch in March 1585, but it took several months for the Estates to consult with their individual provinces and send a delegation to England with a positive response and an offer of sovereignty. Meanwhile, councillors were also discussing various maritime projects 'for annoying of the king of Spain' and redressing the balance of resources between the two realms [107 *p. 55*]. In the spring of 1585 Elizabeth sent ships to attack the Newfoundland fishing fleet, agreed to Sir Richard Grenville's colonizing expedition to Virginia, and gave Drake a provisional licence for a voyage to the West Indies [20; 107; 151].

Rumours of England's privateering plans soon filtered through to Spain. In a panic that the English intended an attack on his treasure ships, Philip took a series of actions, designed to build up a fleet quickly in Portugal, which escalated into an embargo on trade and the seizure of English shipping and goods in Iberian ports in June 1585 [107]. Elizabeth and her councillors, however, wrongly assumed that the ships were seized to augment an invasion fleet. The embargo therefore seemed to vindicate men like Walsingham who had long been arguing that a Catholic league was in existence 'for the ruyne and overthrow' of Protestants [107 *p. 63*]. Furthermore, those merchants who had benefited most from Anglo-Iberian trade and whose attitude to Spain had consequently been ambivalent, at once clamoured for the right of reprisal; the economic arguments in favour of continued peace were forgotten [17].

Nonetheless, the embargo did not materially affect English policy, for the negotiations with the States-General of the Netherlands were already well in train. Although Elizabeth refused to accept their sovereignty, in August and September she signed the Treaties of Nonsuch which committed her to pay for 5,000 foot soldiers and 1,000 horses to be sent to the Netherlands under an English commander. As security for her support and repayment of her expenses she was given control of the towns of Brill and Flushing. At the same time she sent Drake to release the English ships in Spain and raid the ports and shipping of the Caribbean. Despite these provocative actions, Elizabeth still hoped for peace. No sooner had she signed the Nonsuch treaty than she began to extend unofficial peace-feelers to Parma and to reconsider her decision to send troops. Leicester, her chosen commander, sighed with relief when he was at last allowed to go, for 'no man hath had more discouragements' [60 *p. 352*; 2]. Similarly, Elizabeth hesitated to unleash Drake and his fleet until the very last moment. No wonder that when the order to leave finally came, the fleet set sail in some disarray, fearing the order would be revoked, for 'we [were] not the most assured of Her Majesty's perseverance to let us go forward' [19 *p. 98*].

FRANCE 1564–85

In 1564 Elizabeth signed the Peace of Troyes which ended hostilities with France. Thereafter she preferred to remain a bystander to the spectacle of seemingly endless civil wars in France. She no longer tried to exploit French weakness and recapture Calais. War was too expensive and risky, especially as the Huguenots had demonstrated their unreliability as allies in 1563. Unmoved by pleas that they were Protestant brethren in need of her protection, Elizabeth usually appeared more influenced by the fact that, despite their princely titles, the Huguenots were rebels against their lawful sovereign. Nevertheless, Elizabeth could not afford to be an impartial observer of events in France for fear that the Guises might win power at court and exert royal influence on behalf of Mary Stuart. After Mary Stuart's deposition and flight to England in 1568, the Guises were actively trying to rescue her from confinement and restore her to the throne of Scotland. There was the danger too, especially after the 1570 papal bull excommunicating Elizabeth, that they would persuade the French king to back Mary's claim to the throne of England [91; 92].

To deal with this threat Elizabeth acted on several fronts. Whenever possible, she tried to co-operate with the French royal family and detach them from Guise influence. The opening of matrimonial negotiations with Henry Duke of Anjou in 1570 was partly designed to stop both Charles IX from exerting pressure for Mary's release and Anjou from acting as her protector [35]. When these negotiations broke down, discussions were held for an Anglo-French defensive treaty. Elizabeth's commissioners successfully managed to exclude from its terms any mention of Mary's claim to Scotland or a joint commitment to her restoration. Indeed, in signing the Treaty of Blois in April 1572, Charles IX not only explicitly promised not to attack England on grounds of religion but implicitly left Mary Stuart to look after her own future. Even after the massacre of St Bartholomew and the reopening of the French monarch's war against the Huguenots, Elizabeth did not break off relations with the French court, although relations distinctly cooled. She had no wish to drive France into the arms of Spain by displaying a lack of goodwill, and she also hoped to prevent the French from sending troops to Scotland where Mary Stuart's supporters were gaining some ground. She, therefore, allowed talks about a marriage between her and Francis Duke of Alençon to go ahead; although at this time she had no intention at all of wedding him, the negotiations served the useful diplomatic function of keeping lines of communication open despite the French court's policy of taking up arms against her co-religionists [35; 91; 92].

There were times, however, when Elizabeth had to resort to giving undercover aid to the Huguenots in order to ensure their political and military survival. They were granted unofficial help in 1568, through an arrangement whereby the Huguenots at La Rochelle would exchange some of their products for munitions from the English Merchant Adventurers. In 1570, Elizabeth went one stage further and made formal offers of money; three years later she agreed to send secret supplies of munitions to La Rochelle which was under seige from a royal army. From 1585 she subsidized Henry of Navarre [84; 85; 91; 92]. When the danger from the Guises seemed most acute, Elizabeth even considered direct intervention in the French civil wars. In September 1568, she was informed that the Guises were planning to launch an attack on the Huguenot leaders as a preliminary to arranging a marriage between Anjou and Mary Stuart and invading England, possibly with Spanish help. In response, her ambassador told the French court that she would intervene because of 'the duty to her subjects, the friendship she has for the King and the preservation of her own estate' – a message clearly intended as a warning to the cardinal of Lorraine [92 *pp. 168–9*]. In 1575 Elizabeth went much further. With the death of Charles IX the previous year, his brother Henry of Anjou succeeded to the throne. Henry was known in England as a fanatical Catholic and close associate of the Guises. Consequently, when a broad-based coalition of Huguenots, Politiques* and princes of the blood asked Elizabeth to back their bid for power, she agreed, and had not this opposition group been reconciled with Henry III at the Peace of Monsieur, in 1576, she might well have been drawn into the civil wars [44; 60].

The Guise threat not only made Elizabeth take an active interest in French politics, but involved her too in the affairs of Scotland. From 1560 to 1568, French influence in Scotland was at a low point. The success of the 1560 expedition and the eclipse of Guise power in France helped loosen the links between the two realms. Catherine de Medici was unsympathetic to Mary Stuart; she opposed any suggestion of a marriage between Mary and Anjou and after Mary's defeat by her subjects at the battle of Carberry Hill in 1567 she recommended that the queen be confined to a convent. As seen, however, the Guises had other plans for their kinswoman, and the political instability in Scotland after 1570 gave them the opportunities to try to realize them.

The assassination of Regent Moray in January 1570 plunged Scotland into a civil war between the Marians and the adherents of the young King James. The Marians looked to the Guises for military aid while the supporters of James sought help from Elizabeth. Yet Elizabeth did not want to send military aid to the Protestant king's party for several reasons. First, she could not afford a confrontation with France in the aftermath of the Northern Rebellion and at a time when she was quarrelling with Spain. Second, she was still considering whether or not to restore Mary and hence thought it unwise to strengthen the Scottish queen's opponents. On the other hand, under pressure from her Council, she realized that some action was required. 'The Frenche wyll shortely have a grette factyon ther than wylbe fer our proffyte her,' wrote Sussex, who was her President of the Council of the North [158 *p. 274*]. Even worse, the Marians had joined up with fugitive rebels from the 1569 rising and were mounting a series of raids on the English side of the border. Fearing that these were but a preliminary to a full-scale Franco-Scottish invasion, Elizabeth ordered an army into Scotland with the limited purpose of destroying the power of the Scottish border lords and flushing out the English rebels. Accordingly, in April, Sussex raided the Scottish borders, devastated the dales and seized the principal strongholds [158].

However, the military success of the raid was short-lived and it failed completely in its purpose. The English rebels, still in conjunction with their Scottish allies, soon resumed their attacks on the English borders. The king's party remained weak and in disarray; 'the sone's partie daily decayeth, the mother's partie daily increaseth,' wrote Sussex [158 *p. 282*]. The French continued to pose a threat. Just before the raid, there were rumours that a French force was preparing to go to Dumbarton Castle, held by the Marians; immediately afterwards Charles IX demanded the withdrawal of the English troops and announced that if Elizabeth assisted the king's party he would help the Marians.

Elizabeth was still unwilling to give direct aid to the Scottish Protestants but Sussex did not share his queen's reluctance [*Doc. 17*]. On his own initiative, taking advantage of her instructions 'to comforte our party there' and to negotiate a truce, he openly encouraged the king's supporters and offered military support if they assisted him in suppressing the English rebels. As the Marians would not surrender the rebels, he sent troops to Edinburgh in May to join with the Protestant lords assembled there and harass the Marian lords. The queen approved this venture as its ostensible aim was to frighten the Marians into giving up the rebels. However, when the French informed her that there would ensue a kind of war between England and France if she continued to attack the Marians, Elizabeth immediately ordered the withdrawal of her forces and opened discussions for the restoration of Mary [158].

All was quiet for a couple of months. In July, however, the Marians once more challenged the king's party, threatened to call in the French, and resumed their protection of the English rebels who again raided the English borders. Pressed by Sussex to act, Elizabeth agreed to a third incursion across the frontier. To safeguard her negotiations with Mary and to forestall French threats, Elizabeth insisted that Sussex should make his raid look punitive. Nevertheless, she told him that if the limited raid did not bring security to the king's supporters 'we do warrant you to give them ayde of some part of our army' [158 *p. 307*]. This third expedition was the most successful politically. The border lords submitted to Elizabeth and abandoned the rebels, many of whom left Scotland. There was no need for Sussex to use his troops against the Marians, as they too surrendered and agreed to disarm. The French did not intervene.

After this success, Elizabeth tried to withdraw from military involvement in Scotland. She preferred to continue negotiations for the restoration of Mary and to reach a *rapprochement* with France. The Ridolfi plot put an end to her hopes for the former, but the latter was achieved in the Treaty of Blois. Nevertheless, the possibility of a revival of French influence in Scotland remained and was still a matter of concern to Elizabeth's Council. As Burghley pointed out, France could not afford to abandon the Marians and so an Anglophile regent for Scotland was urgently needed to restore order and keep out the French. For this purpose, Elizabeth sent her troops again into Scotland, in November 1572, to capture Edinburgh Castle and thereby to help the pro-English regent, Morton. Once Morton had asserted political control, Elizabeth withdrew from giving further support to his régime for fear that France would break off the entente achieved at Blois. She would neither enter a Protestant league with Morton nor even grant pensions to the Scottish lords to ensure their continued loyalty [86; 97].

Morton dominated Scottish politics, with England's diplomatic support, until 1579. In that year James's cousin Esmé Stuart, Sieur d'Aubigny, arrived in Scotland, won James's favour and engineered Morton's fall and execution (1580–81). These developments alarmed the English government, for D'Aubigny was believed to be a Guise agent working to persuade James to renounce his protestantism, marry a French princess and claim the English throne. Yet despite advice from councillors such as Leicester and Walsingham, Elizabeth would not intervene to save Morton or destroy D'Aubigny. She was afraid that military pressure from England would push the Scots into the arms of the French, as Morton had little support among his own nobility, and that it might lead the French to halt the negotiations she had just initiated for a league against Spain. While Elizabeth waited upon events, D'Aubigny was bringing about his own downfall by quarrelling with the Scottish presbyterian leaders. In August 1582, a group of Protestant lords kidnapped the king in the Ruthven raid and detained his favourite. English agents had paid money over to the conspirators but it is unknown how far Elizabeth's government was implicated in the plot. D'Aubigny, in fear of his life, fled to France but the French were powerless to help him. Elizabeth still needed to disengage James from an independent or pro-French position. This she could not manage until 1585 when James accepted, in principle, the notion of a league with England in return for a pension. After protracted negotiations in 1586 the size of the pension James was to receive from her was fixed at £4,000 a year [60; 86].

Thus Elizabeth, after 1560, consistently demonstrated a marked reluctance to give financial or military aid to the Protestant pro-English party in Scotland. Only extreme pressure from her Council or men on the spot could induce her to give it limited support in 1570, 1571 and 1572. These were times when the threat of French intervention seemed to be greatest. Unlike most of her Tudor predecessors, Elizabeth demonstrated little or no interest in absorbing Scotland into England; perhaps she was aware that the task would be done for her through the succession of James to the English throne.

While it was the Guises and Catholic faction which favoured a forward policy in Scotland, it was their opponents who pursued a policy of military intervention in the Netherlands. There had been secret contacts between the leaders of the French Huguenots and the Netherlands' opposition to Philip II from as early as 1566. In 1568 some 3,000 Huguenots invaded Artois to aid the Prince of Orange, while in 1572 the Huguenot leader, Admiral Coligny, persuaded Charles IX to order a French army into Flanders [73]. Some advisers, like Walsingham and Leicester, regarded the prospect of a Protestant league against Spain with enthusiasm and hoped for English participation. Elizabeth and councillors like Burghley and Sussex, on the other hand, viewed the prospect with alarm. They feared French ambitions and believed that a French presence in the Netherlands would be even more dangerous to England's security than the Spanish one. If the French occupied Flanders they would control the coast from Brittany to Antwerp, threaten English trade and challenge English sovereignty on the narrow seas. Without the communications problems of the Spaniards, the French would be less vulnerable to internal opposition or external attack. A memorandum by Burghley best expressed this viewpoint [*Doc. 18*]. Although Burghley was sympathetic to the Calvinist rebels, he recommended at this point (June 1572) that if the Spaniards were incapable of keeping the French out of the Netherlands, the queen should, given certain conditions, intervene on their side against the French. These precautions were in the event unnecessary, for French aid to the rebels came to nothing. A small French force of 6,000 was wiped out by the Spaniards in July 1572, and the massacre of St Bartholomew in August prevented further French involvement for some years [60].

As Orange was convinced of the urgent need for foreign assistance against Spain, and as English aid was not forthcoming, the rebels appealed once more to the French. It was not until 1578 that they received a positive response, when Francis Duke of Anjou (known as Alençon until 1578), agreed to send troops. To meet the danger, Elizabeth veered towards a well-worn diplomatic manoeuvre. Once she had satisfied herself that Anjou was acting independently of the French government, she decided to woo him into her camp by marriage. In this policy she had the support of only a few of her councillors; Sussex and Burghley were keen advocates, while Lord Hunsdon and Sir Thomas Wilson came out in its favour [*Doc. 20a*]. Leicester and Walsingham, on the other hand, were firmly opposed to it, and had won over most of the Council including Sir Christopher Hatton and Lord Admiral Lincoln by October 1579. Elizabeth, nevertheless, pressed on with the marriage negotiations from the spring of 1578 until the end of 1579. There can be little doubt that she herself was ready to marry. Only when she faced manifestations of popular hostility to the match and the obvious reluctance of her Council to accept it, did she back down [35] [*Doc. 20b*]. By that time, Elizabeth's fears of Spanish power were overtaking her mistrust of French ambitions. Consequently, once she had discarded the idea of marriage as politically impossible, she was ready to negotiate an offensive Anglo-French league against Spain. In September 1580 her ambassador in France raised the question of a league with Henry III and Catherine de Medici, but after some detailed discussions the French insisted upon the marriage as a preliminary to an alliance. In July 1581, Elizabeth sent Walsingham to Paris to offer secret aid for an Anjou expedition to the Netherlands and another proposal for a league against Spain [35]. It was a new direction in Elizabethan foreign policy and was a reaction to the dramatic growth in Spanish power in the years 1579–81. Henry III, however, was unconvinced that Spanish victories constituted a major threat to France's security. Nor was he convinced that Elizabeth was sincere in her offers of aid or a league. As Walsingham reported, Henry feared to commit himself to military action against Spain 'lest when he should be imbarqued, your Majestie would slip the collar' [10 *p. 361*]. Only if Elizabeth were to marry Anjou, as a token of her good faith, would Henry agree to enter a league. This Elizabeth could not do because of domestic policy considerations. Her past record of prevarications and *volte faces* had caught up with her at a critical time.

Although she secured neither the marriage nor the league, Elizabeth nonetheless decided to back Anjou's expedition in the Netherlands. In August 1581, hearing that Henry had refused to provide Anjou with funds, she stepped into the breach. She could not watch passively while the Spaniards reconquered the Netherlands yet she was still not prepared to send English troops there for fear that it would involve her in a lone war against Spain. Anjou had won her confidence, and she believed she could control him. Consequently, she gave him subsidies (£60,000 in 1581–82) and her sponsorship [44]. Anjou, however, was the wrong man for the job. His expedition ended in disaster with an abortive attempt to seize Antwerp, which resulted in the loss of half his men. He returned to France in June 1583 and died there the following year. On his death, Elizabeth tried to persuade Henry III to take on his mantle and aid the Dutch rebels against Spain. As Walsingham wrote, Elizabeth was 'now so convinced of Spanish bad will that she preferred the risks of French domination to Spanish restoration' [60 *p. 307*]. Henry III, however, confronted by the Catholic League at home, was in no position to aid Calvinist rebels against Spain, and Elizabeth ultimately had to act alone.

WAR 1585–1603

No formal declaration of war was made against Spain in 1585, but the Leicester expedition to the Netherlands and Drake's raids in Spain and the West Indies were acts of open warfare. Elizabeth, however, viewed the war as a form of politics by other means, an intensification of diplomatic pressure to convince Philip that England was too powerful either to invade or to ignore. Consequently, she intended her intervention to be as limited as possible. At sea she preferred to rely heavily on the initiative of private sailors and shipowners rather than send a royal navy in force against the Spaniards. On land, she viewed her troops as merely a relief expedition to halt the inexorable progress of Parma and was furious when Leicester, in January 1586, accepted the title of Governor-General [19; 60] [*Doc. 21*]. At the same time, she tried to reach a settlement with Spain and opened up at least five parallel sets of peace negotiations between 1585 and 1588 [103].

Philip II was slow to respond to Elizabeth's provocative actions between 1581 and 1585; it therefore seems clear that he was not seeking a pretext for war. As late as August 1585, he was eschewing Catholic offers of alliance and plans for an invasion of England. By the end of December, however, he had decided upon a campaign against Elizabeth and had begun the lengthy military preparations for an armada [117; 151]. In January 1586, he solicited aid from

Pope Sixtus V for a war 'to subdue that kingdom to the authority of the church of Rome and to give it to the queen of Scots' [151 *p. 9*].

Drake's voyages had not severely damaged the Spanish economy. Philip's comment on the attack on Galicia in northern Spain had been that 'their daring was more impressive than the harm they did' [151 *p. 8*]. In the Indies, Drake's fleet had missed the Spanish treasure ships and had seized booty worth only about £60,000, while Spanish commerce reached a peak in 1585–86. Yet the raids had exposed the vulnerability of Spain's colonial defences and injured her prestige. Leicester's expedition had likewise resulted in no major victory for the rebels. Although his troops recaptured Zutphen and Doesburg (August 1586) and thus secured the Ijssel crossings, Deventer and Zutphen were betrayed to Parma by their English Catholic officers in January 1587, and, in July, Sluys was captured by the Spaniards. Furthermore, Leicester's political manoeuvres served merely to intensify the regional, factional and religious splits within the rebel ranks which weakened the Dutch ability to fight [2; 72; 73]. Yet the very presence of English troops in the Netherlands seemed, at least at first, to help Dutch morale. Philip and Parma both believed that without the arrival of Leicester the rebels would have sought a negotiated settlement. They were thus convinced that the reconquest of the Netherlands could only be achieved once English help was withdrawn. Throughout 1586 and early 1587 plans were formed for the 'Enterprise of England'. Men and munitions were amassed in the summer of 1587; all was ready for an invasion that year. Drake's 1587 raid on Cadiz, where some twenty ships were destroyed, could only postpone the campaign for a year during which the marquis of Santa Cruz sailed after Drake to defend Spanish shipping in the Indies [19; 56; 74; 75].

Philip's aims in launching the Armada were to recover his reputation after the humiliating English sea raids and 'to reduce that realm to our Holy Catholic faith' [151 *p. 22*]. In his belief that he was acting as God's instrument, he felt optimistic that the invasion would encourage the English Catholics to rise, overthrow Elizabeth and welcome his daughter Isabel as their new queen. But the king never lost sight of reality, and he recognized that his victory over Elizabeth might not be complete. He consequently instructed Parma that in these circumstances he should use territorial gains in the south-east of England to negotiate a favourable settlement, which would leave the Dutch isolated and bring religious toleration to English Catholics [74; 151]. The mere threat of the Spanish Armada had secured advantages for Spain. In February 1587, Elizabeth began informal peace discussions with Parma which culminated in the Bourbourg conference in the summer of 1588, while the Estates, suspicious of her intentions, halted their co-operation with the English forces. They also refused to send ships to help to defend England in June 1588. Yet this was not sufficient for Philip II; convinced that God was on his side, he risked his fleet in war determined to defeat England during the first stage in the suppression of the Netherlands [73].

The defeat of the Spanish Armada owed much to the overambitious nature of the project. There were just too many logistical difficulties for the commanders to resolve: how was the duke of Medina Sidonia, commander of the Spanish fleet, to liaise with Parma and effect a rendezvous at sea? How were Parma's barges to evade the Dutch and slip out of harbour? But John Hawkins's work at the navy board must also take some credit for the Spanish defeat. He had helped create an efficient administrative infrastructure that enabled a well-armed, sizable fleet to be quickly assembled, one that was capable of standing up to the Spanish warships [17; 55; 108].

In the short term the English victory rescued the Dutch and saved England but in the longer term it settled nothing. Within ten years the Spanish losses were replaced (it has been calculated that 72 per cent of the larger ships survived both the campaign and journey home), and in 1596, 1597 and 1599 Philip was able to launch future armadas. The war did not come to an end, on the contrary it escalated as Elizabeth ordered operations in France, Portugal and the Atlantic. Politically, however, the launching and defeat of the Armada was a turning-point in English foreign policy. For the first time Elizabeth came to see Philip as a personal enemy, hell-bent on her deposition and the foreign subjugation of her realm. She felt utterly betrayed by his deception in unleashing the Armada at the very time when Parma was disclaiming all knowledge of it at Bourbourg. Consequently, for the next six years she committed herself to offensive action on the Continent as well as to naval expeditions in the Atlantic [61; 99].

Nonetheless, Elizabeth's principal war aims against Spain, unlike those of many of her commanders and advisers, were always limited in scope. She was seeking neither the destruction of Spanish power nor the acquisition of a colonial empire. In war as in peace she aimed at personal and national security. In practical terms, this meant a favourable settlement in the Netherlands, the freedom of the French Channel ports from Spanish control, and the survival of both Spain and France as strong independent powers to act as a check on each other. Consequently, she had no conception of an overall grand strategy to bring Spain to its knees; she did not seriously contemplate an invasion of Spain or Portugal, a full-scale silver blockade, or the seizure of colonial bases [155].

From 1588 until 1594, Elizabeth and her ministers followed a dual military strategy: privateering at sea to finance the expensive land war in France and the Netherlands. English fleets were sent out to intercept Spanish treasure, destroy potential invasion fleets, disrupt Spanish communications, and defend home waters. On land, Elizabeth kept her troops as auxiliaries in the Netherlands and sent some 20,000 men to France from 1589 until 1595 to throw off the Spanish invasion and keep the Channel ports out of the hands of her enemies [19; 61; 99; 106]. There was a sharp change of emphasis in English policy, however, in the middle years of the decade after Henry IV's conversion to Catholicism in 1593, the triumphant run of military successes against the Spaniards which followed in 1594, and the fall of Groningen in June 1594 (the last major Spanish fortress in the northern Netherlands). First, Elizabeth explored avenues to peace and then, when these failed, she tried to disengage from the Continental war. Part of the reason for this change was the queen's perception that England's security was no longer at risk through the Spanish acquisition of the Channel ports or the domination of the northern Netherlands; part was the recognition that English troops were needed in Ireland to crush the Tyrone rebellion in Ulster which had broken out in May 1595 [100; 71]. Elizabeth therefore eluded French attempts to entice her into an enterprise in the Spanish Netherlands, and transferred 2,000 troops from Brittany to Ireland. Even after Calais fell to the Spaniards in April 1596, Elizabeth was prepared to allow only 2,000 troops to go to France and stipulated that they could only be used for garrison duty. In this policy Elizabeth had the support of the two Cecils (Lord Burghley and his son Robert) but the earl of Essex was keenly opposed to it. Imbued with the chivalric ideal, he believed that England's destiny and honour was to act as the champion of a Europe freed from the domination of Spain [136].

Although Elizabeth was unwilling to participate in further expensive campaigns on land, she did allow two major naval enterprises to be launched against Spain in 1595 and 1596. The goal of the first, led by Drake and Hawkins, was the capture of Panama, the isthmus through which Peruvian silver had to pass, but the project ended in failure and the death of both commanders. The second was a pre-emptive strike on the Spanish fleet at Cadiz, a raid which was under the joint command of Essex and Lord Admiral Howard of Effingham. Elizabeth's aim here was the destruction of Spanish towns and shipping and the capture of booty which would finance the expedition. Essex, however, had other plans; he wanted to capture Cadiz and turn it into a permanent English base. In this way he intended 'to hijack the expedition to suit his own view of how England should fight the war' [136 *p. 81*). At one level the expedition was successful as some fifty-seven ships were burnt or captured in the raid and the town of Cadiz was thoroughly looted. At another level, it proved to be a lost opportunity for both the queen and Essex. The attack on the town had allowed the Spanish merchant fleet to avoid capture and plunder; while Howard's refusal to leave a garrison in Cadiz without authority from the queen ended Essex's plan of securing a naval base to cut off Spanish lines of communication with the Baltic and Indies.

In May 1598, the Franco-Spanish war came to an end with the peace of Vervins. A few months afterwards in September Philip II died, and his successor, Philip III showed interest in reaching a peace with England. Elizabeth too favoured peace as did Burghley and Cecil; consequently preliminary talks took place between the two sides in 1598 and 1599. The English terms for peace reflected the queen's war aims: she demanded neither territorial gains nor financial compensation and was also prepared to concede English exclusion from trade in the Spanish colonies. She would not, however, modify her demands on the future of the Netherlands, and insisted that the provinces should be virtually independent even if under the formal sovereignty of Spain. This was unacceptable to the Spaniards who had no intention of including the Dutch in any peace settlement on these terms. Elizabeth would not agree to a bipartite peace until she was certain that the threat from Spain to the independence of the Netherlands and to the security of England was completely over. For the rest of the reign, low-level talks continued between London and Brussels. At the same time, English troops continued to fight in the Netherlands, but at the Estates' expense, and Elizabeth concentrated her resources on suppressing the Tyrone rebellion in Ulster, which had attracted Spanish support [61; 100; 71].

Elizabeth's handling of the war has been criticized by both contemporaries and some historians. In particular, the fiasco of the 1589 Portugal campaign, the debacle of the Rouen expedition 1590–2 and the divided command of the 1596 Cadiz expedition have all been cited as evidence of Elizabeth's weaknesses as a war leader. She has been censured for her excessive caution, her parsimony and her failure to control her commanders. The latter, Dr Haigh believes, was the outcome of her gender: 'A woman could browbeat politicians and seduce courtiers, but she could not command soldiers' [41 *p. 142*]. It is certainly true that Elizabeth was better at diplomacy than war. For example, her characteristic indecisiveness, which had often bought her valuable time in diplomatic negotiations, usually resulted in confusion and lost opportunities during the crises of warfare. Even so, her problems in fighting the war were more complex than Dr Haigh allows.

Elizabeth's caution and parsimony were in large measure due to a realistic assessment of the military resources at her disposal. She was only too well aware of the limitations of her purse and the unpopularity of her expedients to raise necessary sums, and she cut her royal cloak accordingly. She hesitated before making financial commitments, insisted that her allies should pay their share of the cost of campaigns, and she avoided ambitious ventures. The decision to pursue a privateering war rather than to attack the Spanish navy can be seen in the same light. Dependent as she was on private enterprise for her fleets, she had to allow her captains and investors to pursue the type of warfare that would bring them profit as well as strengthen national security [19; 99]. Nonetheless, Elizabeth did not allow her parsimony to dictate her policies to the extent that she did everything by halves; for her campaigns in France in 1589–92 she raised levies to recruit new men and continually overspent her budgets. The war in Brittany cost her at least £191,878; the expenses incurred in Normandy and Picardy amounted to at least £97,461; and her charges in the Netherlands were £100,000 per annum. From the beginning of 1589 until 1595 the total cost of the Continental war reached £1,100,000 [99; 100].

The queen's inadequate resources affected the success of her policies as well as their scope. Dr Lloyd's book, *The Rouen Campaign 1590–92*, amply illustrates how the raising, equipping and transporting of Essex's army soon revealed England's constrained official military capacity and disclosed the risks Elizabeth would run if she tested it too far. She was, therefore, forced to depend on allies whose aims were at variance with hers and with whom communications were difficult and slow [57] [*Doc. 22*]. Similarly, the 1589 Portugal campaign failed because of organizational weaknesses and a serious confusion of aims. These were not the result of personal differences but the corollary of the joint-stock nature of the whole enterprise. Elizabeth had unequivocally ordered her commanders to 'distress' the Spanish warships undergoing re-equipment in the ports of Santander and San Sebastion, so that they would not 'take encouragement in this time of your absence to attempt some what against this our realm of Ireland' [16 *p. xxix*]. The English fleet was then to sail to Lisbon to burn more ships and, if possible, to provoke a popular rebellion against Philip II, and finally it was to occupy the Azores as a base to intercept the Spanish silver ships [98; 99]. Elizabeth, however, was reliant on private captains and investors with more grandiose and greedy aims who ignored her instructions to destroy Spanish shipping in the northern ports and instead went straight to Lisbon via Corunna. In the queen's words, they 'went to places more for profit than for service' [99 *p. 114*]. The result was a fiasco: the Armada fleet was left to be re-equipped, Drake never arrived at the Azores and there was great loss of English lives. The whole expedition cost the queen £100,000. According to Professor Loades, Elizabeth appears to have learned her lesson from this catastrophe. Although she continued to invest in privateering ventures, afterwards she insisted upon a higher degree of royal participation and control whenever major naval expeditions were undertaken [55]. It is significant that Essex could not persuade his comrades on the Cadiz expedition to disobey the queen's instructions and hold onto the town.

Ultimately Elizabeth's objectives were achieved. Spain was bloodied but undefeated. The Southern Netherlands were restored to Spain on a semi-autonomous basis while the northern provinces remained free. France emerged from the civil wars with a monarch sufficiently strong enough to resist both Spain and the most fanatic French Catholics. Protestantism and national independence were safeguarded from foreign threats. Ireland was subdued and foreign influence expelled. Her policies did not achieve all this by themselves; external factors were more important, but the policies undoubtedly helped.

In the past historians have emphasized that the cost of Elizabeth's success was high – perhaps too high. In less than three years, 11,000 soldiers died in France, though from disease and dearth rather than battle. The administrative machinery creaked under the strain of warfare. Anglo-Hispanic trade ground to a halt. The resulting economic and social grievances, it has been argued, bred 'a new and more critical attitude to the central government, to the monarchy itself (and even to the monarch personally)' [97 *p. 92*]. Today, however, historians are impressed that the damage and dislocation were not greater. Given that the war effort was taking place against a backdrop of harvest failures and trade slumps, the government was remarkably successful in raising the troops and organizing supplies. There were complaints aplenty from the localities but 'serious trouble was averted' and the Council 'had managed, just, to finance the war and supply the armies for eighteen years' [103 *p. 383*]. This was no mean achievement!

PART THREE: ASSESSMENT

Foreign policy is more discernible to historians than it was to contemporaries. Reading through the day-to-day ambassadors' reports and Privy Council deliberations on relations with European states, it is easy to be overwhelmed by the amount of seeming trivia which absorbed the time and attention of Tudor governments. Maritime disputes, diplomatic protocol and trading conditions for merchants abroad were but some of the routine business which fill the pages of surviving records. Foreign policy was not a rational working out of political or strategic principles but instead a reaction to the immediate pressure of events, large and small, and it is worth remembering that governments could not always know when a circumstance was significant or when of little importance. Nevertheless, responses to events were not merely *ad hoc* with no reference to underlying goals. The question to be considered here is whether or not consistent goals emerged during the Tudor period.

In very general terms Tudor monarchs shared the same objectives in foreign policy: dynastic security from pretenders, defence from foreign attack, commercial expansion, and the enhancement of their reputations. In these concerns they differed little from their European counterparts. The priorities and strategies of individual monarchs, however, often differed. Whereas Elizabeth viewed with increasing alarm the prospect of hegemony in Europe by any one power, her father had had no such anxieties as long as he was the ally of the dominant power. Hence in the 1520s and 1540s Henry VIII had chosen to ally with Charles V, the strongest ruler in Europe, against France, unlike Elizabeth, who after 1570 tried to league with France against the might of Spain. Whereas Henry VIII enjoyed war as the sport of kings and test of his honour, after 1563 Elizabeth turned away from dynastic adventure and only sent troops to the Continent after 1585 as a defensive measure. The pursuit of economic advantage was also viewed with varying degrees of enthusiasm by different governments. Henry VII was more interested than his son in finding new trade routes and extending overseas trade. Henry VIII was indeed indifferent to trading ventures beyond Europe, while Mary positively discouraged them and Elizabeth's attitude depended on the temperature of her political relations with Spain.

If the *priorities* of foreign policy did not remain constant during the Tudor period, can any consistent evolutionary development of policy be detected?

R. B. Wernham concludes in his book, *Before the Armada* [97], that a pattern can be seen whereby England developed from a Continental to a maritime power. At the beginning of Henry VII's reign, he argues, England had to come to terms with the loss of her Continental empire and with it her traditional role in European affairs. By 1588, England had adapted to the new situation and found herself a new role: expansion across the Atlantic, maritime ascendancy, and a defensive stance based on control of the Channel and opposition to the hegemony in Europe of any one power. This development, he asserts, was consciously brought about by the Tudor monarchs who gradually recognized and responded to the change in England's circumstances. Wernham appreciates that there were crosscurrents such as dynastic considerations, religious concerns and nostalgia for European conquests. Nevertheless, he believes that there still can be discerned a clear picture of a developing policy. However, it is questionable whether this redirection of foreign policy was as conscious at the time as it now seems with hindsight. Tudor monarchs were both slow and reluctant to give up their territorial ambitions in Europe. The lure of the Hundred Years' War continued until well into Elizabeth's reign. Furthermore, the outlook of Tudor governments remained firmly Continental even at the end of the period; their eyes were directed on Italy, Cleves and the Netherlands more than on the Caribbean or Africa. As Wernham himself points out in a later work, 'the Elizabethan war against Spain was first and foremost a continental European War. . . . It involved the whole of western Europe as well as, indeed more than, the Atlantic and Caribbean' [99 *p. vii*]. Moreover, royal patronage of oceanic explorations was not consistent nor was the navy developed systematically and continuously; rather it was built up in fits and starts.

Tudor foreign policy is best considered as a series of discontinuities rather than as one coherent and developing theme. Radical changes of direction took place several times: on the accession of Henry VIII, for the duration of the 1530s, briefly in the early 1550s and then again in the late 1560s. Foreign policy under

Elizabeth (after the early years of her reign) marks the clearest break with the past. She and her ministers thereafter put *what they saw* as national interests before dynastic glory. In doing so they were conscious of the danger from Spain, instead of being blinded by traditional hostility to France.

Their perception of national interests, particularly security but also economic and religious interests, made Elizabethan foreign policy visionary, despite its many shortcomings, and gave it a quality of greatness. It also pointed the way to the future (though not in any clear line of progress), for, as Wernham writes, 'Elizabeth's government, like later English governments all through the succeeding centuries, could not view without very great alarm such a domination of Western Europe by a single over-mighty power' [99 p. 24].

PART FOUR: DOCUMENTS

DOCUMENT 1   THE CLOTH STAPLE AT ANTWERP

This memorandum was written by Sir William Cecil, probably in 1564, at the time of strained relations between England and the Netherlands' government which resulted in an embargo on the cloth trade.

REASONS TO MOVE A FORBEARING OF THE RESTITUTION OF THE INTERCOURSE TO ANTWERP

It is to be confessed of all men that it were better for this realm, for many considerations, that the commodities of the same were issued out rather to sundry places than to one, and specially to such one as the lord thereof is of so great power, as he may therewith annoy this realm by way of a war.

Secondly, it is probable that by the carrying over to Antwerp of such quantity of commodities out of the realm, as of late years is used, the shortness of the return multiplieth many merchants, and so consequently also this realm is overburdened with unnecessary foreign wares. And if the trade thereof should continue but a while, a great part of the treasure of the money of the realm would be carried thither to answer for such unnecessary trifles ... .

Thirdly, it is to be thought that the diminution of clothing in this realm were profitable to the same for many causes. First, for that thereby the tillage of the realm is notoriously decayed, which is yearly manifest in that, contrary to former times, the realm is driven to be furnished with foreign corn, and specially the City of London. Secondly, for that the people that depend upon the making of cloth are of worse condition to be quietly governed than the husband men. Thirdly, by converting of so many people to clothing, the realm lacketh not only artificers, which were wont to inhabit all corporate towns, but also labourers for all common works.

Whereupon it followeth probably that it were profitable for the realm to have some alteration of the great trade of carrying of clothes out of the realm to Antwerp.

From Public Record Office State Papers, SP 12/35/38.

DOCUMENT 2   CONFLICT WITH SPAIN OVER ENGLISH
TRADING AND PRIVATEERING
EXPEDITIONS

(a) The King of Spain opposed English explorations and trading ventures which threatened the Spanish or Portuguese monopolies. Here John Mason, the English ambassador in Spain, was informing Queen Mary's Council of Philip II's hard-line attitude to English voyages to Guinea. The letter is dated 17 December 1553.

I have thought good to signify unto your Lordships that his Majesty thinketh and then thought that oute of doubt that navigation was not be permitted, being the region plainely known to be in th'occupation of the King of Portugal, so as the said navigation might not be maintained without such notable inconvenience as were not expedient to be adventured; and yet being desirous to have our merchants helped as much as with reason they might be, he would travail that the said King of Portugal should take the merchandises by them provided at reasonable prices, which thing I did not then understand to be so far forth as his Majesty had taken order to have it to be put in execution, and therefore took I it not that overture to be a matter utterly resolved, upon which since then I have perceived to be otherwise. His gentle and courteous talk in this case and the declaration with many words of his displeasure that our merchants should by any mean be hindered, caused me somewhat to mistake his meaning and made me to write less peremptorely then I do now perceive his Majesty pleasure was I then should have done, and is that I shall now do, which is that as without injury the saide navigation cannot be continued, so taketh he the condition offered to the merchants to be the best way to save them as much harmless as may be, the quality of the case considered, which he thought your Lordships and the merchants would like accordingly, whereof his Majesty would gladly hear.

From Kervyn de Lettenhove, *Relations politiques des Pays-Bas et L'Angleterre*, Brussels, 1891, vol. 1, p. 11.

(b) The voyages of John Hawkins and Francis Drake particularly aroused the anger of the Spaniards. This report, dated Seville, 7 December 1569, demonstrates that some contemporary observers from overseas believed that Elizabeth was supporting the sailors for her own ends.

From Cadiz this morning came the following news and immediately after it Don Melendez. He relates how John Hawkins the Englishman, who in New Spain last year had such a fight with the Viceroy and Don Francesco de Luxan, General of the Fleet, recently passed Cape St. Vincent with twenty-five well-found ships, among which are stated to be three of seven hundred tons, thirteen of three hundred, and the rest smaller. There he intercepted a ship trying to make its way to the Netherlands and carried it off together with its entire cargo. ... Every one was utterly horrified at these tidings, than which nothing could be worse for the King and the Indian trade, seeing that with a favourable wind Drake must now be close to the Indian Islands (West Indies). At this juncture the ships from New Spain would certainly be loaded up and on their way, so that the Englishman would have them at his mercy. Don Melendez is neither sufficiently armed, nor has he enough equipment and men to face Drake. But the latter knows how much armament he requires and has made all necessary preparations. And the most annoying part of this affair is that this Hawkins could not have fitted out so numerous and so well equipped a fleet without the aid and secret consent of the Queen. This conflicts with the agreement for the sake of which the King sent an Envoy Extraordinary to the Queen of England. It is the nature and habit of this nation not to keep faith, so the Queen pretends that all has been done without her knowledge and desire. The French write that their King Francis, owing to the tricks played on him during his reign by the English, always had on his lips the following epigram:

'Anglicus, Anglicus est cui nunquam eredere fas est,
　　Tum tibi dicit ave, tanquam ah hoste cave.'

From V. Von Klarwill, *The Fugger News-letters 1568–1605*, 2nd series, trans. L. S. R. Byrne, John Lane, The Bodley Head, 1926, pp. 7–8.

DOCUMENT 3　　THE MAKING OF ENGLISH FOREIGN
　　　　　　　　POLICY

(a) Sir Thomas Smith's De Republica Anglorum, written in 1565, provides a contemporary statement on the structure of government in the sixteenth century. Here is his description of the royal prerogative in foreign policy.

The Prince whom I nowe call (as I have often before) the Monarch of Englande, King or Queene, hath absolutelie in his power the authoritie of warre and peace, to defie what Prince it shall please him, and to bid him warre, and againe to reconcile himselfe and enter into league or truce with him at his pleasure or the advice onely of his privie counsell. His privie counsell be chosen also at the Princes pleasure out of the nobilitie or baronie, and of the Knightes, and Esquiers, such and so many as he shal thinke good, who doth consult daily, or when neede is of the weightie matters of the Realme, to give therein to their Prince the best advice they can. The Prince doth participate to them all, or so many of them, as he shall thinke good, such legations and messages as come from forren Princes, such letters or occurrentes as be sent to himselfe or to his secretaries, and keepeth so many ambassades and letters sent unto him secret as he will, although these have a particular oth of a counceller touching faith and secrets administred unto them when they be first admitted into that companie.

From Thomas Smith, *De Republica Anglorum*, ed. Mary Dewar, Cambridge, 1982, p. 85.

(b) This letter from Sir William Cecil to Queen Elizabeth was written in 1559 or 1560 when the Council was divided over the question of whether to give open aid to the protestant lords in Scotland. Cecil, unlike Elizabeth and some other councillors, favoured a forward policy. His letter reveals the limitations of the royal minister in making policy.

It may please your most Excellent Majesty, – With a sorrowfull harte and watery eies, I your poore servant and most lowlye subject, an unworthy Secretory, besech your Majesty to pardon this my lowlye suite, that considering the proceding in this matter for removing of the French out of Scotland doth not content your Majesty, and that I cannot with my conscience gyve any contrary advise, I may, with your Majestie's favor and clemency, be spared to entermeddle therein. And this I am forced to doo of necessitie, for I will never be a minister in any your Majestie's service, whereunto your owne mynd shall not be agreable, for thereunto I am sworne, to be a minister of your Majesty's determynations and not of myne owne, or of others, though they be never so many. And on the other part to serve your Majesty in any thyng that myself cannot allow, must nedes be an unprofitable service, and so untoward, as therin I wold be loth your Majesty should be deceyved. And as for any other service, though it were in your Majesty's kytchen or garden, from the bottom of my harte I am ready without respect of estymation, welthe, or ease, to doo your Majesty's commandement to my lyve's end. Whereof I wish with all my poor sorrowfull hart, that your Majesty would make some proofe, for this I doo affyrme, that I have not had sence your Majesty's reigne, any one daye's joye, but in your Majesty's honor and weale.

From T. Wright, *Queen Elizabeth and Her Times*, London, 1838, vol. 1, pp. 24–25.

DOCUMENT 4   HENRY VII'S TREATY WITH SPAIN, 1489

The Treaty of Medina del Campo was signed by Ferdinand and Isabella on 28 March 1489. But Henry did not finally ratify it until 23 September 1490 when various additional articles were included.

1. A true friendship and alliance shall be observed henceforth between Ferdinand and Isabella, their heirs and subjects, on the one part, and Henry, his heirs and subjects, on the other part. They promise to assist one another in defending their present and future dominions against any enemy whatsoever... .

2. Neither party shall in any way favour the rebels of the other party, nor permit them to be favoured or stay in his dominions.

3. Mutual assistance to be given against all aggressors within three months after the assistance has been requested. The assisted party to pay the expenses, which are to be fixed by four knights, two from each side.

4. Henry is not permitted to assist Charles, King of France, or any other prince at war with Spain. Ferdinand and Isabella promise the same to Henry.

5. Henry is not to conclude peace, alliance or treaties with France, without the sanction of Ferdinand and Isabella, who, on their side, bind themselves to the same effect with respect to Henry.

6. As often as and whenever Ferdinand and Isabella make war with France, Henry shall do the same, and conversely... .

17. In order to strengthen this alliance the Princess Katharine is to marry Prince Arthur. The marriage is to be contracted *per verba de futuro* as soon as Katherine and Arthur attain the necessary age.

From A. F. Pollard, *The Reign of Henry VII from Contemporary Sources*, London, 1913, vol. 1, pp. 2–5.

DOCUMENT 5   **HENRY VII AND BRITTANY**

This dispatch from the Collector de Giglis to Pope Innocent VIII on 28 January 1489 describes Henry's policy towards Brittany.

... his Majesty himself made many loving speeches about your Holiness, saying he had nothing more at heart, than when the preparations of Christendom shall be matured, to proceed against the Infidels; he added that he was not meditating anything against the King of the French, but he is compelled at present to defend the Breton interests, both on account of the immense benefits conferred on him by the late Duke in the time of his misfortunes, and likewise for the defence of his own kingdom; the affairs of Britanny being so bound up with those of England, that the latter are necessarily endangered by the Breton catastrophe; and that he has sent ambassadors to the King of the French for peace, which if effected, all will be well; but if not, he has determined to defend Britanny and the orphan Duchess with all his might.

Ambassadors have also been sent to the King of Castile, to confirm the confederacy which was well nigh concluded here, in which there is a clause about a marriage to be contracted between the only son of the King and one of the daughters of the aforesaid King of Castile.

An embassy has been dispatched to the King of the Romans and the Flemings to arrange matters at issue, or, if that may not be, at least to make friendship with both, or with one or other of them, whichever will consent to fair terms so that trade, so long suspended between the parties, may be brought back into its accustomed channel.

The parliament, which has been summoned, will commence on the 13th of this month. Its chief care will be to make provision for the war, above all the necessary funds for its prosecution – a matter of no small difficulty, as for their acquirement, not only on the laity will a heavy burden be laid, but also on the clergy, who it is said, will be subjected to a tax of three-tenths.

From *Calendar of State Papers Venetian I 1202–1509*, pp. 177–8.

DOCUMENT 6   A FOREIGN OBSERVER'S VIEW OF HENRY VII

... this kingdom is perfectly stable, by reason, first, of the King's wisdom, whereof every one stands in awe; and, secondly, on account of the King's wealth, for I am informed that he has upwards of six millions of gold, and it is said that he puts by annually five hundred thousand ducats, which is of easy accomplishment, for his revenue is great and real, not a written schedule, nor does he spend anything. He garrisons two or three fortresses, contrary to the custom of his predecessors, who garrisoned no place. He has neither ordnance nor munitions of war, and his body guard is supposed not to amount to one hundred men .... He well knows how to temporise, as demonstrated by him before my arrival in this kingdom, when the French ambassadors wanted to go to Scotland under pretence of mediating for the peace, but he entertained them magnificently, made them presents, and sent them home without seeing Scotland; and now he sends one of his own gentlemen in waiting to France. The Pope is entitled to much praise, for he loves the King cordially, and strengthens his power by ecclesiastical censures, so that at all times rebels are excommunicated.

From *Calendar of State Papers Venetian I 1202–1509*, p. 261.

DOCUMENT 7   WOLSEY'S AIMS IN FOREIGN POLICY

In 1518 Wolsey clearly desired peace, but his motives for seeking it are less clear.

(a) LETTER SIGNED 10 MARCH 1518

That it was expedient there should be peace between the Christian powers to which England was much inclined, and especially Cardinal Wolsey, who, when there was a question of hostilities, opposed them strenuously.

From *Calendar of State Papers Venetian II 1509–19*, p. 435.

(b) LETTER SIGNED 24 SEPTEMBER 1518

The Cardinal stated that peace and confederacy would be concluded between the Kings of England and France, the Pope, the Emperor, and the Catholic King. If any one of the allies took up arms or plotted against another of them, all the confederates were bound to defend the latter, at the cost of the petitioner for aid. Knowing the Cardinal to be greedy of glory and covetous of praise, [I] told him that he would obtain immortal fame by this alliance, for whereas the Pope had laboured to effect a quinquennial truce, his Lordship had made perpetual peace, and whereas such a union of the Christian powers was usually concluded at Rome this confederacy had been concluded in England, although the Pope was its head.

From *Calendar of State Papers Venetian II 1509–19*, p. 458.

DOCUMENT 8   **WOLSEY AND THE POPE**

This letter written by the Imperial ambassador in Rome in July 1520 demonstrates the Pope's desire for an English alliance and his strong antipathy to Wolsey.

The Pope is so desirous to conclude the alliance that if he is asked to make the Cardinal his legate in England, and if pressure be brought to bear upon him, he will nominate the Cardinal. Although there is no man on the face of the earth whom his Holiness detests so heartily as the Cardinal, he will be constituted legate if the Pope be given to understand that in no other way can he get out of the difficulties in which he is placed.

From *Calendar of State Papers Spanish 1509–25*, p. 309.

DOCUMENT 9   **HENRY VIII'S AMBITIONS IN FRANCE**

On 26 March 1527, after Francis I's capture and defeat at the battle of Pavia, Henry told his ambassadors in France to congratulate the Emperor and suggest to him the invasion and partition of France.

And in this matter the said ambassadors may say that, the Emperor being contented to make the said personal invasion on that side, such ways may be taken, leving fortresses and strongholds, that the Emperor may come with his army unto Paris, where the King's Highness will not fail, God willing, to meet him; ... At which Paris, after the said personal meeting, the King's Grace may in this case take the crown of France; and the same had, His Grace, to show mutual correspondence of kindness unto the Emperor, shall give unto him all effectual assistance for attaining of his crown Imperial: wherein the said ambassadors shall use these degrees:

First, they shall say the King's Highness can in this case be contented to give the Emperor 5,000 archers at the King's charges, for five, or, rather than fail, for six months, or in the lieu and stead thereof, the sum of 100,000 crowns.

The second degree is, that the said ambassadors shall grant thereunto the sum of 150,000 crowns.

Thirdly, 200,000 crowns: and finally, if by none of these offers the Emperor can be induced to invade in person, meeting the King at Paris as afore, they shall say, as of themselves, that they doubt not but, the crown of France once had, the King's Highness will be contented in his own person to accompany the Emperor unto Rome. And if such general words will not satisfy the Emperor and his Council, the said ambassadors shall not let, all the residue of the King's desire in this point concurring with the same to conclude the King's personal accompanying of the Emperor unto Rome, there to see the crown Imperial set on his head, giving his best assistance as well thereunto, as to the recovery of all such droits and rights as appertain to the Empire, whereof Italy is the chamber: of which glorious voyage the said ambassadors shall say is like to ensue unto the Emperor the whole monarchy of Christendom; for of his own inheritance he hath the realm of Spain, and a great part of Germany, the realms of Sicily and Naples, with Flanders, Holland, Zeeland, Brabant, and Hainault, and other his Low Countries; by election he hath the Empire, whereunto appertaineth almost all the rest of Italy, and many towns imperial in Germany and elsewhere; by the possibility apparent to come by my Lady Princess he should hereafter have England and Ireland, with the title to the superiority of Scotland, and in this case all France with the dependencies: so as the said Emperor, performing this voyage, and taking this way, should in process be peaceable lord and owner in manner of all Christendom; which the King's Grace can be contented the Emperor shall have, he concurring effectually with the King for recovery of his crown of France ....

As to the second, who should succeed in the realm of France, the French King and his line removed? The King's Highness verily trusteth that, his just title and right thereunto remembered and considered, the Emperor, since the treaties and alliances passed between the King's Grace and him, was never, he is, of other mind but firmly to join with His Highness for recovery of the said crown; wherein the said ambassadors may, apart unto himself, put him in remembrance of his secret promise made, as well unto the King's

Highness as to my Lord Legate, at sundry places and times: wherefore in this matter there is no question or ambiguity which may insurge, but that the French King taken or not taken, his army vanquished or not vanquished, one of the chief and principal things intended and convented by their confederation hath always been to expel the French King from his usurped occupation of the crown of France, and to conduce the King's Highness, as right requireth, unto the same ....

From M. St Clare Byrne (ed.), *The Letters of Henry VIII*, Cassell, 1936, pp. 36–7.

DOCUMENT 10   HENRY AND SCOTLAND, 1543–44

(a) Henry's ambassador to Scotland, Sir Ralph Sadler, advised Henry on how to handle the Scottish lords after the English victory at Solway Moss. Henry did not heed the advice. The letter is dated 20 March 1543.

'Well,' quoth I, 'Mr Douglas,[1] the king's majesty hath had large offers, as ye know, both for the government of the realm, and to have the child[2] brought into his hands, with also the strong holds, according to your promises; and if your ambassadors should now come with mean things, not agreeable to his highness, you are a wise man, ye know what may ensue thereof'. 'Why,' quoth he, 'his majesty shall have the marriage offered to be contracted, and they have authority to conclude it; and having that first, the rest of his desires may follow in time. But for my part, quoth he, 'I made no such promise as ye speak of; and they that made such promises, are not able to perform them. For surely,' quoth he, 'the noblemen will not agree to have her out of the realm, because she is their mistress; but they are content, that the king's majesty shall appoint some gentlemen of England, and some English ladies, to be here about her person, for her better tuition, at his majesty's pleasure; and this entry at the first may bring her wholly into his hands in short time; but I tell you,' quoth he, 'all things cannot be done at once.... And again,' quoth he, 'of the other party; if there be any motion now to take the governour[3] from his state, and to bring the government of this realm to the king of England, I assure you, it is impossible to be done at this time. For,' quoth he, 'there is not so little a boy but he will hurl stones against it, and the wives will handle their distaffs, and the commons universally will rather die in it, yea, and many noblemen and all the clergy be fully against it....'

1. Sir George Douglas. A Scot who had been exiled in England but was sent back by Henry VIII to his native country after Solway Moss to strengthen the English party in Scotland.

2. Mary Stuart.

3. James Hamilton, Earl of Arran.

From A. Clifford (ed.), *The State Papers of Sir Ralph Sadler*, Edinburgh, 1809, vol. 1, pp. 69–70.

(b) Henry made clear to the Earl of Hertford the punitive nature of his expedition into Scotland.

It may further like your Lordship tunderstande, that the King's Majestie hath also seen your Devise for the Proclamation, which his Majestic surely thinketh to procede of a good Hart and Will to serve him; and we all think the same. And yet, forasmuch as if ye shulde cause the same to be proclaymed now at your furst entre, before youe wer sure how to fynde those of that Cuntrey, which ought to serve his Majestie, youe cannot then afterward burne and spoyle the Cuntrey with his Majesties Honour, having ones proclaymed his Majestie to be as it wer chief Governour of the Quene and Protector of the Realme; we think it better ye differre the same untill such Tyme, as you shall see that youe have the upperhande of the Ennemys, and the Mastery of the Cuntry in your Hande; and that youe have Experience that suche as shuld be the King's Majesties Freends there do joyne ernestly with youe; which failling youe may fall to burning, having proclaimed nothing openly before, that ought to let youe therefro in Honour. And this is our Advise, which your Lordship may ensue, or otherwise do, as Things shall ministre unto you occasion. Wherof youe, seeing them there at your Eye, shalbe able moche better to judge and use the Commoditye of the same presently, thenne we can here. We returne unto youe the Proclamation agayn, which his Majestie hath altred in one or twoo Things as youe shall perecyve by the same.

From S. Haynes, *A Collection of State Papers Relating to Affairs in the Reigns of King Henry VIII, King Edward VI, Queen Mary and Queen Elizabeth*, London, 1740, p. 21.

DOCUMENT 11   **WILLIAM PAGET'S ADVICE TO SOMERSET AND THE COUNCIL ON FOREIGN POLICY, 28 APRIL 1549**

Albeit I knowe that with out myne advise your grace and the rest of my lordes can determyne the matter proponed by youe the last daye furst apart to me and then in counsaill concerninge your procedinges for Scotland: yet for discharge both of my dewtie of conscience and also bond of service to my soveraigne and countrey, I haue thought good with humble submission of my judgemente to the wisedome of your grace and the rest of my lordes and others of the kinges majesties counsaill to saye myne opinion as foloweth. And furst I thincke that the suertie and honour of the kinges maistiee and the realme is to be preferred above all other things; which surtiee and honour is not to be measured by any one present acte, as to take this or that place, oneles there be also a foresight of a certayne habilitie and power to kepe it stille and to defend throughly all other inconveniences which may grow by occasion of the same, for elles to seke honour by getting of a place, and afterward for lacke to be enforced to lose or leave the same againe, or ells to lose in the meane time some other thinge that shall countervaile two suche as yow thincke to get ys rather a reproche and a dishonour in the world, by whose judgement in meane thinges honour dishonour better and worse is determyned. When Boulogne was wonne the victory semed honourable at the furste and so dyd our entrey into warre after the death of the kinge upon Scotlande. But now having felt the charges of bothe to have bene so great and the inconvenience of them suche as we are not (for any thinge that I knowe) able to avoyde, the moste part of men forthinke the takinge of Boulogne and diverse wise men wishe that we had lived in the surceance of warre with Scotlande. When Boulogne was wonne yt was saide we shuld never have good peace with Fraunce tille yt were restored. And when we beganne warre firste with Scotlande the French kinge said he wolde rather lose his realme then leave them.... Wherfore without peace with Scotlande I beleve that the French kinge will neuer be at peace with Englande. Then yf warre with Scotlande bringe warre with Fraunce, yt is good to consider whether we be hable to maintayne warre with Fraunce so many yeres as we shall make them wery to take parte with Scotlande. And yf we be, then maye we be the bolder to contynewe our conquest and fortifications in Scotlande. But if we be not I thincke we are not then to take more and fortefie more and in thende to be enforced to leave it over to your enemie, albeit the first parte *viz.* takinge, hath a visage of honor: yet the other parte *viz.* after waste of much tyme, spence of much money, losse of your people, to leave to your enemi, that which youe haue gotton, and to the kinge, his owne realme in mysery and beggerye when he shall enter him selfe to governement, ys a certayne and inevitable dishonour in the judgement of the worlde .... Youe do consider I am suer, how great a prince the French kinge ys .... And on the other side how we are exhausted and worne to the bones with these eight yeres warres both of men money and all other thinges for the warres your grace and my lordes knowe better then I, what credyt youe haue to borowe abrode, ... and howe like we are to haue any helpe of your subjectes yow se presently before your eyes. As for the abandoninge of Hadington ys no dishonour but rather a wisedome and so reputed throughe the worlde ... The king that deade is being a prince with longe continuance of great fame & reputacion, upon consideracion of his estate and condition at home could fynde in his herte to forbeare the warres with Scotlande, havinge the same querell that we pretende nowe, and yet was yt no dishonour to him at all. All I suppose (under correction) that if we who haue renewed the warres and wonne by them forbeare now further invasion for a tyme and stand to the defence of so muche of that which we haue wonne of Scotlande as our power will serve to, in respecte of our scarcitie, nother the Scottes nor any other prynce hath cause to thincke dishonour in us, and thoughe they dyd, for want of knowledge of our estate, yet must we do that we maye and are able to do, which me thincketh is very litle.

From B. L. Beer and S. M. Jack (eds.), *The Letters of William, Lord Paget of Beaudesert 1547–1563*, Camden Miscellany (vol. 25), 4th series, vol. 13, 1974, pp. 76–8.

DOCUMENT 12   **MARY'S MARRIAGE TO PHILIP II**

The Spanish ambassador in England frequently warned Philip II of French plots to foil the projected marriage alliance.

It is important that your Highness make speed to come to this kingdom, not merely for the marriage, but for other private and public business. Unless your Highness comes before Lent, I doubt it may be difficult to induce the Queen to marry at that time, though his Majesty has taken steps to obtain the necessary dispensation from the Pope. It is feared that the English people may give trouble in the course of next summer on account of religion and also because they are irritated against the nobility and the Spanish match, but the councillors and principal vassals and nobles approve, provided your Highness comes before spring time and caresses the English with your wonted kindliness. You may be certain that the ill will of the heretics has been exploited by the French, who are fitting out a number of men-of-war on the Breton and Norman coasts with a view to trying to stop your Highness, so you must be accompanied by enough ships to defeat any surprise attack.

From *Calendar of State Papers Spanish 1554–58*, pp. 18–19.

DOCUMENT 13   **THE EARL OF SHREWSBURY INFORMS THE PRIVY COUNCIL OF THE FAILURE OF THE SCOTS TO INVADE ENGLAND, OCTOBER 1557**

It may please your honourable Lordships to be advertised; being in continual expectation, and laying daily wait of the Scots' entry into England; having our force prepared to defend them and annoy them, in such sort as has been signified to your Lordships, and I in readiness, with 1000 men, to have set forwards, and done as the occasion of the enemies' proceeding should have required; the Scots, whose enterprise had been much slacked with foul weather, after many consultations, and full determinations to enter England (being continually pricked forwards thereunto by the Queen and the French) were come the 17th of this instant to Eckford church, upon their driest frontiers towards Wark ... and hereupon encamping that night upon Hawdon Ridge, set forwards the next morning, being the 18th, and came near to Wark, having brought their ordnance over the Tweed; and skirmished before Wark, shewing such a likelihood to have given the approach that the Englishmen within, looking for the siege, had ramparted up the gates; yet that afternoon they brake up their camp, and retired back again and dispersed; and so their enterprise, begun with great bravery, is ended with dishonour and shame, praise be given to God therefore.

From E. Lodge, *Illustrations in British History*, London, 1838, vol. 1, p. 356.

DOCUMENT 14   **THE LOSS OF CALAIS**

Lord Grey of Wilton, Governor of Guisnes, warned Mary of the danger to Calais from the French on 4 January 1558 and informed her of his need for reinforcements.

My most bounden duty humbly premised to your Majesty. Whereas I have heretofore always in effect written nothing to your Highness but good, touching the service and state of your places here; I am now constrained, with woful heart, to signify unto your Majesty these ensuing.

The French have won Newhaven Bridge, and thereby entered into all the Low Country and the marshes between this [Guisnes] and Calais. They have also won Rysbanke, whereby they be now master of that haven.

And this last night past, they have placed their ordnance of battery against Calais, and are encamped at St. Peter's Heath before it: so that I now am clean cut off from all relief and aid which I looked to have (both out of England, and from Calais) and know not how to have help by any means, either of men or victuals.

There resteth now none other way for the succour of Calais and the rest of your Highness's pieces on this side, but a power of men out of England, or from the King's Majesty [Philip II]; or from both, without delay, able to distress and keep them from victuals coming to them, as well by sea as land; which shall force them to leave their siege to the battle, or else drive them to a greater danger.

For lack of men out of England, I shall be forced to abandon the Town [of Guisnes], and take in the soldiers thereof for the Castle. I have made as good provision of victuals as I could, by any means, out of the country; with which, GOD willing! I doubt not to defend and keep this piece as long as any man, whosoever he be, having no better provision, and furniture of men and victuals than I have.

From Edward Arber, *Tudor Tracts, An English Garner*, ed. A. F. Pollard, Cooper Square, New York, 1964, p. 319.

DOCUMENT 15   ENGLISH AID TO THE HUGUENOTS, 1562

(a) This memorandum, dated 20 July 1562, was drafted by Sir William Cecil to draw attention to the dangers to England of a Guise victory in France.

THE PERILLS GROWING UPPON THE OVERTHROW OF THE PRYNCE OF CONDEE'S CAUSE.

The whole regyment of the crowne of Fraunce shall be in the hands of the Guisians; and, to mayntene there faction, they will pleasure the Kyng of Spayne in all that they maye. Hereuppon shall follow a complott betwixt them twoo, to avance there owne pryvat causees; the King of Spayne, to unhable the Howss of Navarr for ever from clayming the kyngdom of Navarr; the Howss of Guife, to promote there nece the Quene of Scotts to the crown of England. And for doing therof twoo thyngs principally will be attempted: the mariadg betwixt the Prynce of Spayne and the sayd Quene; and, in this compact, the realme of Irland to be gyven in a praye to the King of Spayne.

Whylest this is in work, and that the protestants rest as beholders onely; the general counsell shall condemne all the protestants, and gyve the kyngdoms and dominions therof to any other prynce that shall invade them. In this meane tyme, all the papistes in England shal be sollicited not to styrr; but to confirme there faction with comefort, to gather monny, and to be redy to styrr at one instant, when some forrayn force shall be redy to assayle this realme, or Irland.

Whan the matter is brought to these termes, that the papiste shall have the upper hand; than will it be to late to seke to withstand it: for than the matter shall be lyke a great rock of stone that is fallyng downe from the topp of a mountayn, which whan it is comming no force can stey.

Whosoever thynketh, that relentyng in relligion will aswage the Guisians aspirations, they ar farr deceyved: for two appetites will never be satisfyed, but with the thyng desyred; the desyre to have such a kyngdom, as England and Scotland may make unyted; and the cruell appetite of a Pope and his adherents to have his authorité restablished fully, without any new daunger of attempt.

From Patrick Forbes, *A Full View of the Public Transactions in the Reign of Queen Elizabeth*, London, 1741, vol. 2, p. 2.

(b) Elizabeth explained to Philip II on 22 September 1562 some of her anxieties about the political and religious divisions in France.

Surely we have bene much trobled and perplexed from the beginning of these divisions in France, and upon diverse cawses: fyrst, becawse we had a great compassion to see the yong King owr brother so abused by his subjects, as his aucthoritie could not direct them to accord. Next thereto we feared, that herof might followe an universall troble to the rest of christiendome; considering, the quarrell was discovered and published to be for the matter of relligion. Lastly, which towcheth us most nearely and properly, we perceaved, that the Duke of Guise and his Howse was the principall head of one parte; and that they daylie so increased their force, as in the end they became commaunders of all things in France; and theruppon such manner of hostile dealyng used, in diverse sorts, against our subjects and merchants in sondry parts of France, as we were constreyned to looke abowte us, what perill might ensue to our owne estate and contrey.

And thereupon could we not forgett, how they were the very parties that evicted Callice [Calais] from this crowne; a matter of continuall greef to this realme, and of glory to them; and unjustly observyd also the first capitulations, for the reddition thereof into there hand. Nether cold we forgett, how hardly by their meanes we were delt withall at the conclusion of the peace at Casteau in Cambresy [Câteau-Cambrésis].

From *ibid.*, vol. 2, p. 53.

DOCUMENT 16   **THE SPANISH TREASURE SHIPS**

Having asked the Queen and Cecil for the return of the treasure ships to their owners, de Spes reported to Alva their response in a letter dated 22 December 1568 and urged immediate reprisals.

Cecil was very grave about it, as also was the earl of Leicester. Sometimes they said they were guarding it for his Majesty, and sometimes that it belonged to other persons; but they would not say whether they had sent similar orders to Plymouth and Falmouth. Their refusal to declare themselves on the point, however, proves that they have done so. They consulted the Queen and then said that the money was in safe keeping and no other answer could then be given. I pressed for an audience and they told me to ask again after dinner, they in the meanwhile being closeted with the ambassador of the prince of Condé, so that I could get no reply from them. The Chamberlain was requested to go and ask the Queen, which he went in to do at once, and came out very much irritated, saying he had not ventured to ask her Majesty for audience as she was not in the habit of granting it on such days. The affair is thus in a very bad way and these people are determined to do any wickedness, so this money will not be recovered. I pray your Excellency do not fail to seize all English property and send word to Spain instantly for them to do the same there.

From *Calendar of State Papers Spanish 1568–79*, p. 91.

DOCUMENT 17   SCOTLAND, 1570

Sussex's first raid into Scotland was ostensibly to punish the Scottish Marian lords harbouring the English rebels who had fled after their abortive rising in 1569. Sussex here was urging Cecil to persuade the Queen to make a decision on further action. He wanted to give aid to the protestant lords against the Marians but Elizabeth found difficulty in determining future policy.

The time passeth away, and therefore it were good her Majesty would resolve what she will do; for as if she will restore the S. Q. it were no good policy to have me shew countenance on the other side, so, if she will maintain the other side, and command me to join with them, I will, with allowance of 300 carriage horses, make all men within 30 miles of the borders to obey that authority, or I will not leave a stone house for any of them to sleep in in surety that shall refuse; and, if her Majesty command me to pass further, I will, with the help of Morton,[1] deliver the castle of Edinburgh, or any other in Scotland, to the hands of any in Scotland whom Morton, with her Majesty's consent, shall appoint to receive them. These matters have too long slept; it is time now to wake; and, therefore, good Mr Secretary, sound the Queen's mind fully; and if she intend to restore the Scotch Queen, advise her to do it in convenient sort, and suffer me not to put my finger in the fire without cause, and her to be drawn into it by such degrees as are neither honourable nor sure; and if she will set up the other side, and make open shew thereof, let her command what she will, and it shall be done, or I will lie by it.

1. Morton; James Douglas 4th Earl of Morton, one of the Lords of the congregation, became Regent at the end of 1572.

From E. Lodge, *Illustrations of British History in the Reign of Elizabeth*, London, 1838, vol. 1, p. 506.

DOCUMENT 18   THE NETHERLANDS, 1572

In this 'Memorial for Matters of Flanders' drawn up in June 1572, Burghley expressed his concern that the French should not obtain a foothold in the Netherlands.

If upon these and other intelligences it appear manifest that the Duke of Alva is sufficiently prepared and able to resist all attempts, so as he may detain his master's countries from the conquest of the French, then it is like to be best for England to let both sides alone for a time; otherwise the French may be offended and the Spaniard not made sure, and if they accord we shall be sure of neither.

If it appear that the Duke is not able to defend his master's countries from the French and that the French begin to possess any part of them, and especially the maritime parts, then it is like that the French, increasing their dominance, may be too potent neighbours for us and therefore [it] may be good for us to use all the means that may conveniently be, to stay that course.

If the French proceed to seek to possess the maritime coasts and frontiers it seemeth to be good that by some good means the Duke of Alva were informed secretly of the Queen's Majesty's disposition to assist the king his master by all honourable means she might in the defence of his inheritance, so as it may appear to her that he will discharge his subjects of their intolerable oppression, restore them to their ancient liberties, reconcile his nobility to him, deliver them from the fear of the Inquisition and continue with her Majesty the ancient league for amity and traffic in as ample sort as any others, dukes of Burgundy, heretofore have done.

From Kervyn de Lettenhove, *Relations politiques des Pays-Bas et L'Angleterre*, Brussels, 1891, vol. 6, p. 421.

DOCUMENT 19   THE NETHERLANDS, 1578

Walsingham, Elizabeth's ambassador to the Estates in the summer of 1578, wrote regularly to his fellow councillors of events in the Netherlands, in the hope that they might urge Elizabeth to intervene – but to no avail.

(a) WALSINGHAM'S LETTER TO SUSSEX DATED 23 JULY 1578

For what case things stand here and what will become of these countries in case Her Majestie withdraws her promised assistance from them, we have so largely set down in our general letter to Your Lordship and the rest of My Lords as I think it needless to make any recital therof. Truly, my Lord, if Her Majesty do not presently resolve to take an other course then I perceive (to my great grief) she is inclined to, I see apparently that this country will become french.

From *ibid.*, vol. 10, p. 631.

(b) LEICESTER'S LETTER TO WALSINGHAM DATED 1 AUGUST 1578

I am sorry to see both our travail fall out to no better effect. Good Mr Secretary, it grieveth me, I cannot say how much, that I am neither able to satisfy that expectation in you I would most gladly, nor yet take comfort my self in our proceeedings here. It is no small alteration I find in Her Majesties disposition, since we were at Otland and Windsor, toward the state of those countries. How loth she is to come to any manner of dealings that.way, specially to be at any charges, it is very strange.

From *ibid.*, vol. 10, p. 678.

DOCUMENT 20   **THE ANJOU MARRIAGE SCHEME, 1578**

The Council was divided over the proposed marriage.
(a) Sussex was its leading proponent, as he demonstrates in this letter to Elizabeth.

Touching the marriage (if your Majesty in your own heart can like of it, which I leave to God and you) I find these commodities to follow. Your alliance with the house of France; whereby (besides all likelihood that the French King will not attempt any thing to the prejudice of you and his brother) you shall be assured, by yourself and your husband, to have such a party in France as the French King shall not be able, nor shall not dare, to attempt directly or indirectly any thing against you. You shall, by yourself, and your husband, be able to assure the Protestants of France from peril of massacre by the Papists, and the King from any perilous action by them; and so, by your means, keep the King and his people in unity and Christian peace. You shall take away, and suppress, all practise for competition,[1] for Popery, or any other seditious cause, at home or abroad; and so shall, at home and abroad, assure your person, and your state, from all perils that by man's judgement might grow any ways to you by France. You shall, also, by the help of your husband, be able to compel the King of Spain to take reasonable conditions of his subjects in the Low Countries, and the States to take reasonable conditions of their King, so as he may have that which before God and man doth justly belong to him, and they may enjoy their liberties, freedoms, and all other things that are fit for their quiet and surety .... And herewith, for the more surety of all persons and matters, yourself may have in your own hands some maritime port, to be by you kept, at the charge of the King of Spain; and your husband may have some frontier towns in like sort; and both to be continued for such a number of years as may bring a settling of surety to all respects; by which means you shall also be delivered from perils, at home and abroad, that may grow from the King of Spain. And if you like not of this course in dealing for the Low Countries, you may join with your husband, and so, between you, attempt to possess the whole Low Countries, and draw the same to the Crown of England if you have any child by him; or, if you have none, to divide them between the realms of England and France as shall be meetest for either; but, to be plain with your Majesty, I do not think this course to be so just, so godly, so honourable, nor, when it is looked into the bottom, so sure for you and your State as the other, although at the first sight it doth perhaps carry in shew some plausibility.

1. Competition for the succession to the Crown of England: alluding to the pretensions of the Queen of Scots.

From E. Lodge, *Illustrations of British History in the Reign of Elizabeth*, London, 1838, vol.2, pp. 109–11.

(b) Amongst the body of writings against the marriage was a famous letter written by Philip Sidney, Leicester's nephew.

As for this man, as long as he is but Monsieur in might and a Papist in profession, he neither can nor will greatly stead you. And if he grow king, his defence will be like Ajax' shield, which weighed down rather than defended those that bore it.

Against contempt at home, if there be any, which I will never believe, let your excellent virtues of piety, justice and liberality daily, if it be possible, more and more shine. Let some such particular actions be found out (which is easy, as I think, to be done) by which you may gratify all the hearts of your people. Let those in whom you find trust, and to whom you have committed trust in your weighty affairs, be held up in the eyes of your subjects. Lastly, doing as you do, you shall be as you be: the example of princes, the ornament of this age, the comfort of the afflicted, the delight of your people, the most excellent fruit of all your progenitors, and the perfect mirror to your posterity.

From K. Duncan-Jones and J. Van Dorsten (eds), *Miscellaneous Prose of Sir Philip Sidney*, Oxford University Press, 1973, pp. 56–57.

DOCUMENT 21   LEICESTER'S INSTRUCTIONS FOR HIS
EXPEDITION TO THE NETHERLANDS,
DECEMBER 1585

To have care that her majesties subjectes serving under his lordship maie be well governed, and to use all good meanes to redresse the confused government of those countreys, and that some better forme might be established amongst them.

Touchinge the good ruling of her majesties subjectes, his lordship is directed to bend his course, during his charg there, rather to make a defensive then an offensyve warr, and not in any sort to hazard a battaile without great advantage ....

To lett the states understand, that, where by their commissioneres they made offer unto her majestie, first, of the soueraintie of those countreyes, which for sundrie respects she did not accept, secondlie, unto her protection, offring to be absolutelie governed by such as her majestie wold appoint and send ouer to be her lieftenant. That her majestie, although she would not take soe much uppon her as to comaund them in such absolute sort, yet unlesse they should shew themselves forward to use the advise of her majestie to be delivered unto them by her lieftenaunte, to work amongst them a faire unitie and concurrence for their owne defence, in liberall taxacions and good husbanding of their contribucions, for the more speedie atteyninge of a peace, her majestie wold think her favours unworthelye bestowed upon them.

To offer all his lordships travaile, care, and endevour, to understand their estates, and to geve them advice, from tyme to tyme, in that which maie be for the suretie of their estate and her majesties honour.

From J. Bruce (ed.), *Correspondence of Robert Dudley, Earl of Leycester 1585 and 1586*, Camden Society, 27(1844), pp. 12–15.

DOCUMENT 22   **ENGLISH AID TO HENRY OF NAVARRE**

Henry of Navarre was here replying to Elizabeth's request for a place in Brittany to act as a supply base for the English troops assisting him against Spain.

Considering the humours of some of his Catholic councillors, he could not assent to yielding Brest or St. Malo in particular, but would conclude that the first port town to be taken from the enemy should be delivered to Her Majesty for the retreat of her people. He hoped the Queen would not now forsake him, knowing how far she was interested in the common cause. He knew well what would immediately result for England if the Spanish King became King of France. 'Her Majesty made war at this time good cheap against so great enemy ... and [he] wished that he had such another fool as Her Majesty had of him to make wars against the King of Spain, that he might look out at the window, as she doth now, and behold the tragedies between him and his enemies now in action.' He also knew how much it would import her to have so evil a neighbour as the Spaniard in Brittany. He was unwilling to lose so fair a part of his kingdom and he would do all he could to defend it.... Henry wanted to know whether the Queen might be moved to send him 2,000 men more for one month, in case Parma should return to give him battle. Wilkes and Unton said that she was disposed rather to revoke those already in France. The King said that with such help he would undertake to overthrow Parma and take Rouen, whereby he might draw into his purse 300,000 *livres* yearly over and above his present revenue. By settling the traffic there he would be able to furnish himself at all times with money to supply his extremities.

From R. B. Wernham (ed.), *List and Analysis of State Papers, Foreign Series, Elizabeth I*, vol. 3, June 1591–April 1592, p. 380, paragraph 665, HMSO.

MAPS

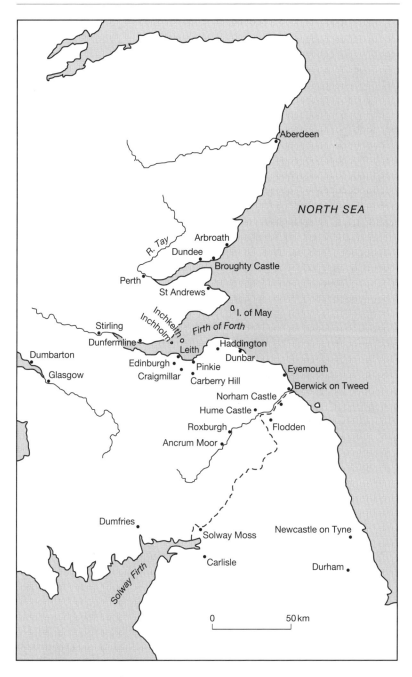

Southern Scotland and the Border

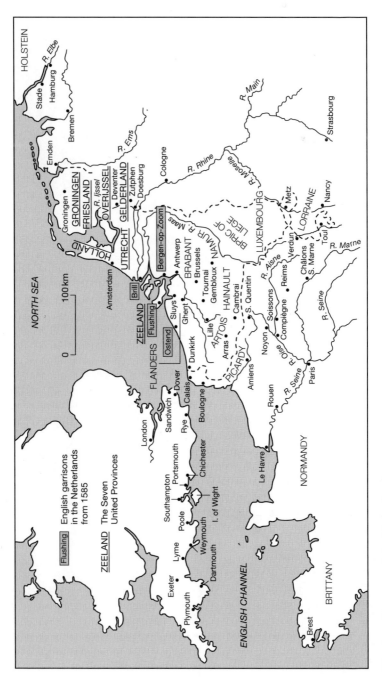

Northern France and the Netherlands

CHRONOLOGY

1485   Battle of Bosworth (Aug.). Truce signed with France (Oct.).

1486   Three-year truce with James III of Scotland. Commercial treaty with Brittany (July).

1487   Lambert Simnel crowned Edward VI in Ireland. Battle of Stoke (June).

1488   Accession of James IV of Scotland (June). French victory in Brittany. Death of Duke Francis of Brittany (Sept.).

1489   Treaty of Redon with Brittany (Feb.). Anglo-Spanish Treaty of Medina del Campo (March). Yorkshire rebellion.

1490   English troops in Brittany.

1491   Perkin Warbeck in Ireland. Defeat of Breton resistance. Marriage of Anne of Brittany to Charles VIII (Dec.).

1492   Invasion of France (Oct.). Treaty of Étaples (Nov.).

1493   Warbeck welcomed in Flanders. Embargo on trade with the Netherlands.

1495   Warbeck's attempted invasion at Deal (July). Warbeck's arrival in Scotland.

1496   *Magnus Intercursus* (Feb.). Henry joined Holy League. Scottish raid over the border (Sept.). Declaration of War against Scotland.

1497   Cornish rebellion. Seven-year truce of Ayton with Scotland (Sept.). Commercial treaty with France.

1499   Execution of Warbeck (Nov.).

1501   Marriage of Prince Arthur and Catherine of Aragon (Nov.).

1502   Death of Arthur (April). Treaty of Ayton with Scotland (Sept.).

1503   Death of Queen Elizabeth (Feb.). Anglo-Spanish matrimonial treaty (June). Marriage of James IV and Margaret Tudor (Aug.).

1504   Death of Isabella of Castile (Nov.). Earl of Suffolk's arrival in the Netherlands.

1505	Trade sanctions on the Netherlands (Jan.).
1506	Arrival of Philip of Burgundy in England (Jan.). Treaty of alliance agreed (Feb.). *Malus Intercursus* (April). Death of Philip (Sept.).
1508	League of Cambrai (Dec.).
1509	Accession of Henry VIII (April). Marriage to Catherine of Aragon. Wolsey appointed Almoner.
1510	Wolsey on Council. Renewal of truce with France.
1511	Holy League against France (Nov.). Anglo-Spanish agreement to attack France.
1512	Declaration of war against France (April). English campaign in Gascony.
1513	Army royal sent to northern France. Siege and surrender of Thérouanne. Battle of the Spurs (Aug.). Defeat of Scots at Flodden and death of James IV (Sept.). Siege and surrender of Tournai.
1514	Anglo-French peace-treaty (Aug.).
1515	Wolsey appointed Lord Chancellor. Accession of Francis I and his victory at Marignano.
1516	Death of Ferdinand of Aragon and accession of Charles (Jan.). Franco-Spanish Treaty of Noyon (Aug). Birth of Princess Mary.
1517	Agreement between Francis and Maximilian.
1518	Treaty of London (Oct.).
1519	Death of Maximilian (Jan.). Election of Charles as Holy Roman Emperor (June).
1520	Henry's meeting with Charles V in England (May). Field of Cloth of Gold (June). Meeting with Charles at Calais.
1521	Outbreak of hostilities between Francis and Charles. Wolsey meets with Francis I at Calais and Charles V at Bruges (Aug.). Anglo-Imperial Treaty.
1522	Declaration of war against France (May). Surrey expedition in Picardy.
1523	Treason of duke of Bourbon. Suffolk's unsuccessful march on Paris.
1525	Imperial victory at battle of Pavia (Feb.). Instructions to levy 'Amicable Grant' (March). Charles V's refusal of partition of France. Anglo-French Treaty of the More (Aug.).

1526   League of Cognac against Charles V (May).

1527   Henry VIII's search for an annulment. Anglo-French Treaty of Westminster (April). Imperial sack of Rome (May). Treaty of Amiens (Aug.).

1528   Declaration of War against France (January).

1529   Defeat of French at Landriano (June). Peace of Cambrai (Aug.). Fall of Wolsey (Oct.).

1530   Death of Wolsey (Nov.).

1531   Thomas Cromwell admitted to inner Council.

1532   Defensive alliance with France (June).

1533   Secret Boleyn marriage (Jan.). Anne crowned queen (May). Franco-papal accord.

1534   Act of Supremacy.

1535   Negotiations with Schmalkaldic League.

1536   Execution of Anne Boleyn (May). Outbreak of Pilgrimage of Grace.

1537   Birth of Prince Edward.

1538   Franco-Imperial Truce of Nice (June). Papal excommunication (Dec.).

1539   Invasion scare. Act of Six Articles. Cleves matrimonial negotiations.

1540   Cleves marriage (Jan.) and annulment (July). Renewal of Habsburg-Valois disputes in Italy. Fall of Cromwell (April).

1541   Henry's progress to the North and planned meeting with James V.

1542   War against Scotland (Aug.). Battle of Solway Moss (Nov.). Death of James V and accession of his infant daughter, Mary.

1543   Anglo-Imperial alliance (Feb.). Treaties of Greenwich (July). Scottish repudiation of treaties (Dec.).

1544   Hertford's punitive raid into Scotland (May). Army royal sent to France (June). Capture of Boulogne (Sept.). Anglo-French Peace of Crépy (Sept.).

1545   Landing of French troops in Scotland (May). Naval engagements in Solent.

1546   Anglo-French Peace of Ardres (June).

1547   Death of Henry VIII and accession of Edward VI (Jan.). French troops sent to Scotland (Jan.). Death of Francis I and accession of Henry II (March). Somerset's invasion of Scotland (Sept.). Defeat of Scots at battle of Pinkie.

1548   Landing of 10,000 French troops in Scotland (June). Mary Stuart sent to France (July).

1549   English rebellions. French declaration of war against England (Aug.). Fall of Somerset (Oct.).

1550   Anglo-French Treaty of Boulogne: restoration of Boulogne to French (March).

1551   Anglo-French Treaty of Angers (July).

1553   Death of Edward VI. Accession of Mary I (July). Habsburg matrimonial negotiations.

1554   Wyatt's rebellion (Jan.). Marriage of Mary and Philip (July).

1555   Attempt at La Marque to arrange general peace (May). Abdication of Charles V. Partition of Empire.

1557   Renewal of Habsburg-Valois fighting in Flanders (Jan.). Stafford's raid on Scarborough Castle (April). Declaration of War against France (June).

1558   Loss of Calais (Jan.). Dauphin married Mary of Scotland (April). Death of Mary I and accession of Elizabeth I (Nov.).

1559   Treaty of Câteau-Cambrésis (March). Elizabethan Church Settlement (April). Protestant rebellion in Scotland (May). Death of Henry II and accession of Francis II (July). French reinforcements sent to Scottish regent. Conciliar debates on English intervention (Dec.).

1560   English military intervention in Scotland. Treaty of Berwick offering protection to Scottish Lords (Feb.). Treaty of Edinburgh and withdrawal of French troops from Scotland (July). Death of Francis II and accession of Charles IX under regency (Dec.).

1561   Return of Mary to Scotland (Aug.).

1562   Outbreak of first Civil War in France (March). Treaty of Hampton Court with Huguenots (Sept.). English occupation of Le Havre and Dieppe.

1563   Surrender of Le Havre to French (June). Embargo on English trade to the Netherlands (Nov.).

1564   Anglo-French Treaty of Troyes (April). Resumption of Habsburg marriage negotiations.

1566   Political and religious unrest in the Netherlands.

1567   Mary Stuart's abdication (July). Arrival of Spanish army under Alva in the Netherlands (Aug.). Hawkins's third voyage to West Indies (Oct.). End of Habsburg matrimonial negotiations (Dec.).

1568   Mary's flight to England (May). Appointment of De Spes as ambassador to England (June). 'Massacre' of Hawkins's men at San Juan D'Ulua (Sept.). Seizure of Genoese treasure ships. Alva's embargo (Dec.).

1569   Elizabeth's counter-embargo (Jan.). Northern Rising (Oct.).

1570   Assassination of Regent Moray in Scotland (Jan.). Papal bull of excommunication (Feb.). English army raids into Scotland. Negotiations for Mary's restoration.

1571   Anglo-French matrimonial negotiations. Discovery of Ridolfi plot. Civil War in Scotland (Sept.). Battle of Lepanto (Oct.).

1572   Anglo-French Treaty of Blois (April). Expulsion of Sea Beggars and their capture of Brill (April). Massacre of St Bartholomew (Aug.).

1573   Secret aid to La Rochelle. Convention of Nymegen and resumption of Anglo-Spanish trade (March). Fall of Edinburgh Castle to Anglo-Scottish force (May).

1574   Death of Charles IX and accession of Henry III (May). Anglo-Spanish Convention of Bristol (Aug.).

1575   Elizabeth rejected sovereignty of Netherlands (Nov.).

1576   Peace of Monsieur in France (May). Spanish sack of Antwerp. Pacification of Ghent (Nov.).

1577   Perpetual Edict (Feb.) and withdrawal of Spanish troops from Netherlands (April). Drake's voyage of circumnavigation (Nov.).

1578   Spanish victory over rebels at battle of Gembloux (Jan.). Duke of Anjou's negotiations with Dutch rebels. Anjou matrimonial negotiations.

1579   Reconciliation of southern Netherland's provinces with Philip II (May). Papal-backed expedition to Ireland (July). Anjou's visit to England (Aug.). D'Aubigny's arrival in Scotland (Sept.).

1580   Fall of Regent Morton in Scotland. Philip II's successful invasion of Portugal (Aug.). Return of Drake (Sept.).

1581   Drake knighted by queen (Apr.). Anjou subsidized by queen in Netherlands (Sept.). Anjou's Second visit to England (Nov.).

1582   Anjou's expedition to Netherlands (Feb.). Ruthven Raid (Aug.). Parma's victories in Flanders and Brabant.

1584   Death of Anjou (June). Assassination of William of Orange (July). Treaty of Joinville between Philip and Catholic League (Dec.).

1585   Treaty of Nonsuch (Aug.). Drake's expedition to Caribbean (Sept.). Leicester's expedition to Netherlands (Dec.).

1586   Treaty of Berwick: James VI's acceptance of English pension (July).

1587   Execution of Mary Stuart (Feb.). Drake's raid on Cadiz (April).

1588   Defeat of Spanish Armada.

1589   Portugal expedition. Assassination of Henry III and accession of Henry IV (July). War of succession in France. English troops sent to Normandy (Sept.).

1590   Spanish landing in Brittany.

1591   English expedition to Brittany. Siege of Rouen.

1592   Death of Parma (Dec.).

1593   Henry IV's conversion to Catholicism (July).

1594   Henry IV's occupation of Paris and coronation.

1595   Tyrone rebellion. Panama expedition of Drake and Hawkins.

1596   Cadiz expedition.

1598   Treaty of Vervins (May). Death of Philip II and accession of Philip III (Sept.).

1601   Spanish landing at Kinsale (Sept.).

1602   Surrender of Spanish in Ireland (Jan.).

1603   Death of Elizabeth (March).

GLOSSARY

Cortes The representative institution of each of the kingdoms of Spain and Portugal.

Curia Court

Estates–General The national representative assembly.

Fief Territory held in vassalage.

General Council of the Church An assembly of the most important representatives of the church, held irregularly, to discuss reform. In the mid-fifteenth century the Council held at Basle usurped the authority of the pope; henceforeward popes treated the call for a General Council with great suspicion.

Hanse A league of North German and Baltic trading towns.

Huguenots French Calvinists.

Letters of marque Authorisation granted by governments to sea captains which allowed them to attack enemy shipping. Those who held and used letters of marque were *privateers*; those without them who plundered ships were *pirates*.

Malcontents A group of Catholic rebels in the Southern Netherlands who looked to the duke of Anjou to help them in their struggle against the Spanish government.

Merchant Adventurers The company of London Merchants who had a monopoly of trade in cloth to the Netherlands.

Politiques A group of moderates in France during the civil wars who supported the monarchy and opposed extreme Protestantism and Catholicism alike.

Sea Beggars Exiles from the Netherlands who attacked the ships and supporters of the duke of Alva.

Stadtholder The lieutenant governor of provinces in the Netherlands.

Staple A town appointed by royal authority in which a group of merchants had exclusive rights of purchase over certain classes of goods to be exported.

BIBLIOGRAPHY

The bibliography has been brought up to date but some of the references in the first edition have been omitted. It includes in the main only works referred to in the text.

PRINTED PRIMARY SOURCES

1   Brewer, J.S. et al., *Letters and Papers, Foreign and Domestic, of the Reign of Henry VIII*, 21 vols, 1862–1910; Addenda, 1929–32.
2   Bruce, John, *Correspondence of Robert Dudley, Earl of Leycester 1585 and 1586*, Camden Society, 27 (1844).
3   *Calendar of State Papers, Foreign, Edward, Mary and Elizabeth*, (eds) W. Turnbull and J. Stevenson, 1861–63.
4   *Calendar of State Papers Relating to Scotland and Mary, Queen of Scots, 1547–1603*, (ed.) J. Bain, 1898–1969.
5   *Calendar of State Papers Spanish*, (ed.) G. A. Bergenroth, P. de Gayángos and M. A. S. Hume, 1862–99.
6   *Calendar of State Papers Venetian*, (ed.) R. Brown and G. C. Bentinck, 1864–90.
7   *Cabala, Sive Scrinia Sacra*, 1691.
8   Clifford, A. (ed.), *The State Papers and Letters of Sir Ralph Sadler*, 2 vols, Edinburgh, 1809.
9   *A Collection of Scarce and Valuable Tracts ... of the Late Lord Somers*, 2nd edn, (ed.) Walter Scott, vol. 1, London, 1809.
10 Digges, Dudley, *The Compleat Ambassador*, etc., London, 1655.
11 Hay, D. (ed.), *Anglica Historia by Polydore Vergil*, Camden Society, 3rd series, 74, 1950.
12 Haynes, Samuel, and Murdin, William (eds), *Collection of State Papers ... Left by William Cecil, Lord Burghley*, 2 vols, London, 1740–59.
13 Kervyn de Lettenhove, *Relations politiques des Pays-Bas et L'Angleterre...*, 11 vols, Brussels, 1888–1900.
14 Lodge, E., *Illustrations of British History*, 3 vols, London, 1838.
15 Pollard, A. F., *The Reign of Henry VII from Contemporary Sources*, 3 vols, Longman, 1913–14.
16 Wernham, R. B. (ed.), *Expedition of Sir John Norris and Sir Francis Drake to Spain and Portugal 1589*, Navy Records Society, vol. 127, 1988.

SECONDARY SOURCES: BOOKS

17   Adams, Simon, *The Armada Campaign of 1588,* New Appreciations in History, 13, London, 1988.

18   Alexander, Michael van Cleave, *The First of the Tudors: A Study of Henry VII and His Reign,* London, 1981.

19   Andrews, K. R., *Elizabethan Privateering: English Privateering During the Spanish War 1585–1603,* Cambridge, 1964.

20   Andrews, Kenneth R., *Trade, Plunder and Settlement: Maritime Enterprise and the Genesis of the British Empire, 1480–1630,* Cambridge, 1984.

21   Arthurson, Ian, *The Perkin Warbeck Conspiracy 1491–1499,* Stroud, 1994.

22   Beer, Barrett L., *Northumberland: The Political Career of John Dudley,* Ohio, 1974.

23   Bell, Gary M., *A Handlist of British Diplomatic Representatives 1509–1688,* London, 1990.

24   Bennet, Michael, *Lambert Simnel and the Battle of Stoke*, Gloucester, 1987.

25   Bernard, G. W., *War, Taxation and Rebellion in Early Tudor England: Henry VIII, Wolsey and the Amicable Grant,* Brighton, 1986.

26   Bush, M. L., *The Government Policy of Protector Somerset,* London, 1975.

27   Chambers, D. S., *Cardinal Bainbridge in the Court of Rome 1509–1514,* Oxford Historical Series, 2nd series, Oxford, 1965.

28   Chrimes, S. B., *Henry VII,* London, 1972.

29   Connell-Smith, C., *Forerunners of Drake: A Study of English Trade with Spain in the Early Tudor Period,* London, 1954.

30   Corbett, J. S., *Drake and the Tudor Navy,* 2 vols, 2nd edn, London, 1898.

31   Crowson, P. S., *Tudor Foreign Policy,* London, 1973.

32   Cruickshank, C. G., *Elizabeth's Army,* Oxford, 1966.

33   Cruickshank, C. G., *Army Royal. Henry VIII's Invasion of France 1513,* Oxford, 1969.

34   Cruickshank, C. G., *The English Occupation of Tournai 1513–19,* Oxford, 1971.

35   Doran, Susan, *Monarchy and Matrimony: The Courtships of Elizabeth I,* London, 1996.

36   Ferguson, Arthur B., *The Chivalric Tradition in Renaissance England,* London, 1986.

37   Gammon, S. R., *Statesman and Schemer: William, First Lord Paget, Tudor Minister,* Newton Abbot, 1973.

38   Gunn, S. J., *Early Tudor Government 1485–1558,* London, 1995.

39   Guy, John, *Tudor England,* Oxford, 1988.

40   Gwyn, Peter, *The King's Cardinal: The Rise and Fall of Thomas Wolsey,* London, 1990.

41 Haigh, Christopher, *Elizabeth I: Profile in Power*, London, 1988.
42 Harbison, E. Harris, *Rival Ambassadors at the Court of Queen Mary*, London, 1940.
43 Hill, D. J., *A History of Diplomacy in the International Development of Europe*, New York, 1962.
44 Holt, Mack P., *The Duke of Anjou and the Politique Struggle during the Wars of Religion*, Cambridge, 1986.
45 Hoskins, W. G., *The Age of Plunder: The England of Henry VIII, 1500–1547*, London, 1976.
46 Jones, Norman, *Faith By Statute: Parliament and the Settlement of Religion*, Cambridge, 1982.
47 Jordan, W. K., *Edward VI: The Young King*, London, 1968.
48 Jordan, W. K., *Edward VI: The Threshold of Power*, London, 1970.
49 Kourie, E. I., *England and the Attempts to Form a Protestant Alliance in the late 1560s: A Case-study in European Diplomacy*, Helsinki, 1981.
50 Lander, J. R., *Government and Community: England 1450–1509*, London, 1980.
51 Loach, Jennifer, *A Mid-Tudor Crisis?* New Appreciations in History 25, London, 1992.
52 Loades, D. M., *Two Tudor Conspiracies*, Cambridge, 1965.
53 Loades, D. M., *The Reign of Mary Tudor: Politics, Government, and Religion in England 1553–58*, London, 1979, 1991.
54 Loades, D. M., *Mary Tudor: A Life*, Oxford, 1989.
55 Loades, D. M. *The Tudor Navy: An Administrative, Political and Military History*, Aldershot, 1992.
56 Lockyer, R., *Henry VII*, London, 2nd edn, 1983.
57 Lloyd, H., *The Rouen Campaign 1590–92: Politics, Warfare and the Early-Modern State*, Oxford, 1973.
58 Lloyd, T. H., *England and the German Hanse, 1157–1611: A Study of their Trade and Commercial Diplomacy*, Cambridge, 1991.
59 MacCaffrey, Wallace T., *The Shaping of the Elizabethan Regime*, London, 1969.
60 MacCaffrey, Wallace T., *Queen Elizabeth and the Making of Policy 1572–88*, London, 1981.
61 MacCaffrey, Wallace T., *Elizabeth I: War and Politics, 1588–1603*, Oxford, 1992.
62 MacKenney, Richard, *Sixteenth-Century Europe: Expansion and Conflict*, Basingstoke, 1993.
63 Maltby, William, *The Black Legend in England: The Development of Anti-Spanish Sentiment, 1558–1660*, S. Carolina, 1971.
64 Martin, Colin and Geoffrey Parker, *The Spanish Armada*, London, 1988.
65 Mattingly, G., *Renaissance Diplomacy*, London, 1955.
66 Mattingly, G., *The Defeat of the Spanish Armada*, London, 1959.
67 Millar, Gilbert John, *Tudor Mercenaries and Auxiliaries 1485–1547*, Virginia, 1980.

68   Merriman, R. B., *Life and Letters of Thomas Cromwell,* 2 vols, Oxford, 1902.
69   Neale, Sir John, *Elizabeth I and her Parliaments,* 2 vols, London, 1953.
70   Palliser, D. M., *The Age of Elizabeth: England under the Later Tudors, 1547–1603,* London, 1983.
71   Palmer, William, *The Problem of Ireland in Tudor Foreign Policy 1485–1603,* Woodbridge, 1994.
72   Parker, G., *The Army of Flanders and the Spanish Road 1567–1659,* Cambridge, 1972.
73   Parker, G., *The Dutch Revolt 1548–1648,* London, 1977.
74   Parker, G., *Ten Studies: Spain and the Netherlands 1559–1659,* London, 1979.
75   Parmiter, G. de C., *The King's Great Matter: A Study of Anglo-Papal Relations, 1527–1534,* London, 1967.
76   Pollard, A. F., *Henry VIII,* London, 1951 edn.
77   Pollard A. F., *Wolsey,* London, 1929.
78   Pollard, A. F., *England under Protector Somerset,* London, 1900.
79   Prescott, H. F. M., *Mary Tudor,* London, 2nd edn, 1952.
80   Quinn, D. B. and A. N. Ryan, *England's Sea Empire 1550–1642,* London, 1983.
81   Ramsay, G. D., *The City of London in International Politics at the Accession of Queen Elizabeth,* Manchester, 1975.
82   Ramsey, G. D., *The Queen's Merchants and the Revolt of the Netherlands,* Manchester, 1986.
83   Ramsey, P., *Tudor Economic Problems,* London, 1963.
84   Read, Conyers, *Mr Secretary Walsingham and the Policy of Queen Elizabeth,* 3 vols, Oxford, 1925.
85   Read, Conyers, *Mr Secretary Cecil and Queen Elizabeth,* London, 1965.
86   Read, Conyers, *Lord Burghley and Queen Elizabeth,* London, 1965.
87   Redworth, Glyn, *In Defence of the Catholic Church: The Life of Stephen Gardiner,* Oxford, 1990.
88   Scarisbrick, J. J., *Henry VIII,* London, 1968.
89   Starkey, David (ed.), *Henry VIII, A European Court in England,* London, 1991.
90   Storey, R. L., *The Reign of Henry VII,* London, 1968.
91   Sutherland, N. M., *The Massacre of Saint Bartholomew and the European Conflict 1559–1572,* Basingstoke, 1973.
92   Sutherland, N. M., *The Huguenot Struggle for Recognition,* Yale, 1980.
93   Tittler, R., *The Reign of Mary I,* London, 1983.
94   Tjernagel, N. S., *Henry VIII and the Lutherans,* Concordia, St Louis, 1965.
95   Warren, John, *Elizabeth I: Religion and Foreign Affairs,* London, 1993.
96   Weightman, Christine, *Margaret of York, Duchess of Burgundy, 1446–1503,* New York, 1989.

97 Wernham, R. B., *Before the Armada: The Growth of English Foreign Policy 1485–1588*, London, 1966.

98 Wernham, R. B., *The Making of Elizabethan Foreign Policy*, Berkeley, California, 1980.

99 Wernham, R. B., *After the Armada: Elizabethan England and the Struggle for Western Europe 1588–95*, Oxford, 1984.

100 Wernham, R. B., *The Return of the Armadas: The Last Years of the Elizabethan War Against Spain 1595–1603*, Oxford, 1994.

101 Wilkie, W. E., *The Cardinal Protectors of England: Rome and the Tudors before the Reformation*, Cambridge, 1974.

102 Williams, P., *The Tudor Regime*, Oxford, 1979.

103 Williams, Penry, *The Later Tudors 1485–1603*, Oxford, 1995.

104 Wilson, C., *Queen Elizabeth and the Revolt of the Netherlands*, London, 1970.

SECONDARY SOURCES: ARTICLES AND ESSAYS

105 Adams, Simon, 'The Queen Embattled' in Simon Adams (ed.), *Queen Elizabeth, Most Politick Princess*, London, 1984.

106 Adams, Simon, 'The Lurch into War', *History Today*, May, 1988.

107 Adams, Simon, 'The Outbreak of the Elizabethan Naval War against the Spanish Empire: the embargo of May 1585 and Sir Francis Drake's West Indies Voyage' in M. J. Rodriguez-Salgado and Simon Adams (eds), *England, Spain and the Gran Armada 1585–1604*, Edinburgh, 1991.

108 Adams, Simon, 'New Light on the "Reformation" of John Hawkins; the Ellesmere naval survey of 1584', *English Historical Review*, 105, 1991.

109 Adams, Simon, 'The Gran Armada: 1988 and after', Review Article, *History*, 76, 1991.

110 Adams, Simon, 'Favourites and Factions at the Elizabethan Court' in Ronald G. Asch and Adolf M. Birke (eds), *Princes, Patronage and the Nobility: The Court at the Beginning of the Modern Age*, Oxford, 1992.

111 Arthurson, Ian, 'The King's Voyage into Scotland: the war that never was' in *England in the Fifteenth Century: Proceedings of the 1986 Harlaxton Symposium*, Woodbridge, 1987.

112 Arthurson, I., 'The Rising of 1497: a revolt of the peasantry?' in Joel Rosenthal and Colin Richmond (eds), *People, Politics and Community in the Later Middle Ages*, Gloucester, 1987.

113 Beer, B. L., 'The Myth of the Wicked Duke and the Historical John Dudley', *Albion*, 11, 1979.

114 Bell, Gary, M., 'Elizabethan Diplomacy: the subtle revolution' in Malcolm R. Thorp and Arthur J. Slavin (eds), *Politics, Religion and Diplomacy in Early Modern Europe, Sixteenth Century Essays and Studies*, 27, Kirksville, Missouri, 1994.

115   Bernard, G. W. and R. W. Hoyle, 'The Instructions for the Levying
       of the Amicable Grant, March 1525', *Historical Research*, 67, 1994.
116   Calvar, J., 'Summary report' in P. Gallagher and D. W. Cruickshank
       (eds), *God's Obvious Design: Papers for the Spanish Armada
       Symposium Sligo 1988*, London, 1990.
117   Chambers, D. S., 'Cardinal Wolsey and the Papal Tiara', *Bulletin of
       the Institute of Historical Research*, 38, 1965.
118   Cooper, J. P., 'Henry VII's Last Years Reconsidered', *Historical
       Journal*, 2, 1959.
119   Croft, P., 'Trading with the Enemy 1585–1604', *Historical Journal*,
       32, 1989.
120   Croft, P., 'English Commerce with Spain and the Armada War,
       1558–1603' in M. J. Salgado and Simon Adams (eds), *England,
       Spain and the Gran Armada 1585–1604*, Edinburgh, 1991.
121   Currin, John M., ' "Pro Expensis Ambassatorum": diplomacy and
       financial administration in the reign of Henry VII', *English
       Historical Review*, 108, 1993.
122   Currin, John, 'Pierre Le Pennec, Henry VII of England and the
       Breton Plot of 1492: a case-study in "diplomatic pathology" ',
       Albion, 23, 1991.
123   Currin, John, 'The Treaty of Redon ....', *History*, forthcoming.
124   Davies, C. S. L., 'England and the French War, 1557– 9', in J. Loach
       and R. Tittler (eds), *The Mid-Tudor Polity* c. 1540–1560, London,
       1980.
125   Dawson, Jane E., 'Sir William Cecil and the British Dimension of
       Early Elizabethan Foreign Policy', *History*, 74, 1989.
126   De Lemar Jensen: 'The Spanish Armada: the worst-kept secret in
       Europe', *The Sixteenth-Century Journal*, 19, 1988.
127   Dunlop, David, 'The "Masked Comedian": Perkin Warbeck's
       adventures in Scotland and England from 1495 to 1497', *The
       Scottish Historical Review*, 70, 1991.
128   Englebrecht, Jörg, 'Anglo-German Relations in the Reign of Henry
       VIII' in Uwe Baumann (ed.), *Henry VIII in History, Historiography
       and Literature*, Frankfurt am Main, 1992.
129   Elton, Geoffrey, 'War and the English in the Reign of Henry VIII' in
       Lawrence Freedman, Paul Hayes and Robert O'Neill (eds), *War,
       Strategy and International Politics: Essays in Honour of Sir Michael
       Howard*, Oxford, 1992.
130   Glasgow, Jr, Tom, 'The Navy in Philip and Mary's War 1557–1559',
       Mariner's Mirror, 53, 1967.
131   Glasgow, Jr, Tom, 'The Maturing of Naval Administration,
       1556–1564', *Mariner's Mirror*, 56, 1970.
132   Goring, J. J., 'Social Change and Military Decline in Mid-Tudor
       England', *History*, 60, 1975.
133   Gunn, S. J., 'The Duke of Suffolk's March on Paris in 1523', *English
       Historical Review*, 101, 1986.

134 Gunn, Steven, 'The French Wars of Henry VIII' in J. Black (ed.), *The Origins of War in Early-Modern Europe,* Edinburgh, 1987.

135 Gunn, S. J., 'Wolsey's Foreign Policy and the Domestic Crisis of 1527–8' in S. J. Gunn and P. Lindley (eds), *Cardinal Wolsey, Church, State and Art,* Cambridge, 1991.

136 Hammer, Paul E. J., 'Patronage at Court, Faction and the Earl of Essex', in John Guy (ed.), *The Reign of Elizabeth I: Court and Culture in the Last Decade,* Cambridge, 1995.

137 Head, David M., 'Henry VIII's Scottish Policy: a reassessment', *The Scottish Historical Review,* 61, 1982.

138 Horie, H., 'The Lutheran Influence on the Elizabethan Settlement 1558–1563', *The Historical Journal,* 34, 1991.

139 Kouri, E. I., 'Elizabethan England and Europe: 40 Unprinted Letters from Elizabeth I to Protestant Powers', *Bulletin of the Institute of Historical Research,* Special Supplement no. 12, November 1982.

140 Kourie, E. I., 'For True Faith or National Interest? Queen Elizabeth and the Protestant Powers' in E. I. Kourie and Tom Scott (eds), *Politics and Society in Reformation Europe,* London, 1987.

141 Lowe, Ben, 'Peace Discourse and Mid-Tudor Polity' in Paul A. Fideler and T. F. Mayer (eds), *Political Thought and the Tudor Commonwealth: Deep Structure, Discourse and Disguise,* London, 1992.

142 Mayer, Thomas F., 'A Diet for Henry VIII: The Failure of Reginald Pole's 1537 Legation', *Journal of British Studies,* 26, 1987.

143 McKee, A., 'Henry VIII as Military Commander', *History Today,* June, 1991.

144 Merriman, Marcus, 'Realm and Castle: Henry VIII as European Builder', *History Today,* June, 1991.

145 Nolan, John S., 'The Muster of 1588', *Albion,* 23, 1991.

146 Potter, D. L., 'The Treaty of Boulogne and European Diplomacy 1549–50', *Bulletin of the Institute of Historical Research,* 55, 1982.

147 Potter, David, 'Foreign Policy' in Diarmaid MacCulloch (ed.), *The Reign of Henry VIII: Politics, Policy and Piety,* London, 1995.

148 Ramsay, G. D., 'The Foreign Policy of Elizabeth I' in Christopher Haigh (ed.), *The Reign of Elizabeth I,* London, 1984.

149 Ramsey, G. D. 'The Settlement of Merchant Adventurers at Stade' in E. I. Kouri and Tom Scott (eds), *Politics and Society in Reformation Europe,* London, 1987.

150 Richardson, Glenn, 'Good Friends and Brother? Francis I and Henry VIII', *History Today,* September, 1994.

151 Rodriguez-Salgado, M. J., 'The Anglo-Spanish War: the final episode in the "Wars of the Roses"?' in M. J. Rodriguez-Salgado and Simon Adams (eds), *England, Spain and the Gran Armada 1585–1604,* Edinburgh, 1991.

152 Russell, Elizabeth, 'Mary Tudor and Mr Jorkins', *Historical Research,* 63, 1990.

153   Sutherland, N., 'The Foreign Policy of Queen Elizabeth, the Sea Beggars and the Capture of Brill, 1572' in N. Sutherland, *Princes, Politics and Religion, 1547–1589,* London, 1984.
154   Weikel, A., 'The Marian Council Revisited', in J. Loach and R. Tittler (eds), *The Mid-Tudor Polity c. 1540–1560,* London, 1980.
155   Wernham, R. B., 'Elizabethan War Aims and Strategy', in S. T. Bindoff *et al.,* (eds), *Elizabethan Government and Society,* London, 1961.

UNPUBLISHED THESES

156   Adams, Simon, 'The Protestant Cause: religious alliance with the European Calvinist communities as a political issue in England 1585–1630', Oxford D. Phil., 1973.
157   Campbell, Dana Scott, 'English Foreign Policy 1509–21', Cambridge University Ph.D., 1980.
158   Doran, S. M., 'The Political Career of Thomas Radcliffe, 3rd Earl of Sussex (1526?–1583)', London University Ph.D., 1977.
159   Leiman, M., 'Sir Francis Walsingham and the Anjou Marriage Plan 1574–81', Cambridge University Ph.D., 1989.
160   Macmahon, L., 'The English Invasion of France, 1544', Warwick MA, 1992.
161   McEntegart, R., 'England and the League of Schmalkalden 1531–1547: faction, foreign policy and the English Reformation', London University Ph.D., 1992.
162   Potter, D. L., 'Diplomacy in the Mid 16th Century: England and France 1536–1550', Cambridge University Ph.D., 1973.
163   Richardson, Glenn John, 'Anglo-French Political and Cultural Relations during the reign of Henry VIII', London University Ph.D., 1995.

INDEX

RELATED TITLES

Roger Lockyer, *Henry VII* Second Edition (1983)   0 582 35410 2

Henry VII's reign saw the triumph of the crown and the restoration of good order and government after the turbulence of the Wars of the Roses. But Roger Lockyer, in this perceptive analysis of the rule of the first Tudor, shows how Henry worked within existing traditions rather than breaking with the past. At the same time as he brought a new vigour and effectiveness to the royal administration, he preserved much of the medieval structure of both state and church.

M. D. Palmer, *Henry VIII* Second Edition (1984)   0 582 35437 4

The reign of Henry VIII witnessed a dramatic transformation of the early Tudor church and state. M. D. Palmer analyses the changes that took place and also considers the effect upon society of the English Reformation and the dissolution of the monasteries. He concludes with an examination of Henry's character and an assessment of how far he was responsible for the transformation with which his name is identified.

Robert Tittler, *Mary I* Second Edition (1991)   0 582 06107 5

'[a] highly competent survey of the way government functioned in the sixteenth century, which emphasises the role of institutions and the development of policy .... The chapter on the propaganda battles of the reign is a valuable introduction to a complicated subject.'

History Today (of the First Edition)

Professor Tittler addresses the deceptively simple question of whether Mary's reign was really, as some historian claim, just 'a sterile interlude' in Tudor history. It is a balanced account of the reign: Robert Tittler acknowledges the negative aspects of Mary's rule but he also points to its more positive features. He argues that some of these, particularly in religion, came to nothing because of Mary's untimely death; others were brought to fruition by Mary's successor, Elizabeth I, who claimed the credit.

Michael A. R. Graves, *Early Tudor Parliaments 1485–1558* (1990)
0 582 03497 3

This excellent short survey looks at the workings of parliament under the first four Tudor monarchs. After an introductory first section which looks at parliament's medieval origins, the author then considers all aspects of early parliamentary history – including the historiography of the early Tudor parliaments, membership and attendance, the legislative roles of the Lords and Commons and the specific parliaments themselves.

Michael A. R. Graves, *Elizabethan Parliaments 1559–1601*
Second Edition (1996)   0 582 29196 8

A concise and accessible introduction to the parliaments of Elizabeth I. For the Second Edition the author has updated the historiographical debate, provided an extended bibliography, and illustrated the more important political, organisational and functional aspects of the parliaments in the collection of documents. No book can provide the last word on Elizabethan parliaments, but this is certainly the latest word.

Anthony Fletcher and Diarmaid MacCulloch, *Tudor Rebellions*
Fourth Edition (1997)   0 582 28990 4

An important study of the rebellions of the period which throws light on some of the main themes of Tudor history: the dynasty's attempt to bring the north and west under the control of the capital, the progress of the English Reformation in the counties far from London and the impact of inflation, taxation and enclosure on society. Considered by many as a classic in the series the book is now in its Fourth Edition. On Professor Fletcher's invitation Diarmaid MacCulloch has undertaken a major revision of the text, thereby taking into account the scholarship which has appeared since the Third Edition was published in 1983.

W. J. Sheils, *The English Reformation 1530–1570* (1989)

0 582 35398 X

Covering the Reformation and its progress through the reigns of Henry VII, Edward VI, Mary and the early years of Elizabeth, this study analyses the principal reforms, examining their origins by looking at the challenges posed by traditional dissent, humanistic teaching and the growth of continental protestantism. The author considers how the changes were received by different social groups and in different areas, and uses documents to illustrate the main themes and the range of evidence from which historians construct an analysis of the Reformation.

Andrew Foster, *The Church of England 1570–1640* (1994)

0 582 35574 5

'The general reader can enjoy this book as well as the sixth former and undergraduate profit from it.'   *Teaching History*

Dr Foster traces the eventful history of the Church of England from shortly after its establishment in Elizabeth I's reign down to 1640, when it was on the verge of destruction. As well as analysing its principal features he considers the conflicting interpretations that this most controversial of periods has stimulated. He also provides a detailed chronological chart to help readers with alternative readings of events and to prompt thoughts about how 'facts shift according to different perspectives'.